PEREGRINE FALCONS

PEREGRINE
FALCONS

CANDACE SAVAGE

Foreword by Adrian Forsyth

Sierra Club Books
San Francisco

Originally published in Canada by Douglas & McIntyre Ltd., 1615 Venables Street, Vancouver, British Columbia, Canada V5L 2H1

Library of Congress Cataloging-in-Publication Data

Savage, Candace Sherk, 1949–
    Peregrine falcons / Candace Savage.
        p.   cm.
    Includes bibliographical references.
    ISBN 0–87156–504–8 : $30.00
    1. Peregrine falcon.   2. Peregrine falcon—Pictorial works.
    I. Title.
    QL696.F34S28   1992
    598.9'18—dc20   92-2681
                                                              CIP

Production by Jane McHughen
Editing by Barbara Pulling
Jacket design by Alexandra Hass
Book design by Alexandra Hass
Photographs copyright © 1992 by the photographers credited

Printed and bound in Singapore

10 9 8 7 6 5 4 3 2 1

To
Louise C. Savage
and
Robert M. Savage,
with gratitude

CONTENTS

ACKNOWLEDGEMENTS

This book might have been possible without the assistance of Paddy Thompson, but it wouldn't have been as credible nor as interesting. As the co-ordinator for the Saskatchewan Cooperative Falcon Project at the University of Saskatchewan, Paddy has a breadth and depth of knowledge about falcons and falconry that he was always ready to share with generosity. Not only did he patiently put up with my many questions, intrusions at the falcon barn and frequent requests to go out hawking, he also reviewed a version of the manuscript.

I am also grateful to Dr. Lynn Oliphant of the Department of Veterinary Anatomy at the University of Saskatchewan (the director of the falcon project) for conversations that helped me to get my bearings in the complex and controversial world of peregrine research. He encouraged me to see the peregrine story not as the rags-to-riches saga of an avian superstar but as a warning about the impact of pesticides on the web of life.

Special acknowledgement must also be made of several individuals who provided information and advice and who, like Paddy, reviewed portions of the manuscript. They are: Dr. Tom J. Cade, peregrine researcher, World Center for Birds of Prey, Boise, Idaho; Mr. Stan Cuthand, cultural consultant, formerly with the Saskatchewan Indian Cultural Centre, Saskatoon, Saskatchewan; Dr. David Ellis, peregrine researcher, Institute for Raptor Studies, Laurel, Maryland; Dr. Doug Forsyth, wildlife toxicologist, Canadian Wildlife Service, Saskatoon,

Saskatchewan; Mr. Derek Ratcliffe, peregrine researcher, Cambridge, England; Dr. Pierre Mineau, wildlife toxicologist, Canadian Wildlife Service, Ottawa, Ontario; Dr. Robert Nero, peregrine researcher, Manitoba Department of Natural Resources, Winnipeg, Manitoba, and Dr. Brian Walton, peregrine researcher, Predatory Bird Research Center, Santa Cruz, California.

Cheryl Sihoe of Douglas & McIntyre and the ever-cheerful, ever-efficient Tania Spak of Saskatoon both worked long and hard to help assemble the photographs for this volume. Richard Clarke read and re-read early drafts of the manuscript and refused to let me quit until I had it right. He and my daughter, Diana Savage, kept me sane through successive revisions. Alex Hass of Three Design Associates and Barbara Pulling and Rob Sanders of Douglas & McIntyre brought their usual competence and dedication to the whole undertaking.

To all of these people, and to the dozens of others who enriched the book with their knowledge, insights and enthusiasm, I offer sincere thanks.

FOREWORD

A friend of mine, a budding ornithologist, returned from a recent bird-watching excursion with more than her usual enthusiasm. She had been watching a pond full of waterfowl when a peregrine suddenly appeared. The falcon stooped low over the pond, stirring a flock of ducks to flight. As the ducks rose and flapped away in confusion, the falcon wheeled sharply back behind the flock and dropped down on an old squaw. The peregrine struck the duck with outstretched talons, in the same motion grasping the stunned bird and carrying it effortlessly away. Within seconds the falcon was perched with its meal underfoot. My friend is a vegetarian and takes no pleasure from killing. But her excitement was understandable: to witness a hunting peregrine is to see one of evolution's finest achievements in action.

The peregrine is a fierce, uncompromising bird with razor-sharp vision and talons to match. Diving at more than 200 kilometres an hour, this falcon knows no living equal for speed. It is at home nesting on rocky arctic crags where humans have never trod, but a city skyscraper or even an open peat bog will serve as well. Wherever in the world there is open sky, space to nest and prey to hunt, peregrines can be found. But though they are widespread, peregrines, like tigers, are always rare. To see one is a privilege.

The last place I saw a peregrine was in the Kitlope wilderness area of the Coast Mountains of British Columbia. I was perched on top of a windswept ridge. As I stared out across a scene of steep granite gorges capped with glaciers, a peregrine rocketed by me, riding the wind on its long, narrow, raked-back wings. It was gone in an instant, but it had been enough to send a spike of adrenalin through me. The falcon is the perfect bird for a vast wide land of wild rock, river and stormy sky.

It is fitting that organisms such as peregrines, the species that stir the human spirit, are also the species that give the measure of ecosystem integrity. Conservationists recognize the flagship qualities, the special significance, that species such as the peregrine hold for people. They are emblematic of the most wild and rugged, yet most fragile and rare, places left on Earth.

Our admiration and concern for these birds is both aesthetic and pragmatic. The peregrine is a bird with a naturally long life. But sensitive, high-level predators such as peregrines feed at the top of the food chain, and so have served as bellwethers to alert us to the invisible contamination of our world. It is because we have lost large numbers of raptors, including peregrines, that we discovered the progressive poisoning of our food chains by chlorinated hydrocarbon pesticides.

This admirable book extols the natural majesty of peregrines and recounts the history of our relationship with these birds. As you read you may be surprised to learn, as I was, that even peregrines of remote wilderness areas suffer the taint of human pollution. Peregrines range widely during their winter migration. The pesticides manufactured in North America and sold in South America pass from field to stream to diatom to snail to duck, eventually coming home to roost in our northern wilderness. DDT and its relatives cause eggshell thinning in raptors and may adversely affect even those birds that breed thousands of kilometres from any agricultural field. Even falcons undisturbed and alone in the arctic fastness, though they may have food in abundance and a cliff-face aerie a thousand metres beyond the range of predators, sadly lay eggs that crack.

Peregrines, like people, are global organisms. They live everywhere. This account of the falcon's fortunes gives us moving illustration of the interconnection between humans and the other species that share the same ecosystems. It describes the commitment we have made to repairing the damage, to rebuilding the populations of peregrines.

Candace Savage gives us an exploration, a celebration and a call to action. Hers is a voice full of empathy for the natural beauty epitomized in these special birds and full of hope for the future. Read her; admire the images; follow her bidding.

Adrian Forsyth

© WAYNE LYNCH

THE WAYS OF ETERNITY

"I HAVE BROUGHT THE WAYS OF ETERNITY TO THE
TWILIGHT OF THE MORNING. I AM UNIQUE IN MY
FLIGHT."

—Words of the Egyptian falcon god,
from an ancient text

A pair of peregrine falcons is somewhere nearby, probably just across the river on the Bessborough Hotel. Eagerly, I scan the building's craggy, fairy-tale turrets, which spike above the shadows into the high dawn light. No sign of my birds.

It is early and the air is bright, one of those crystal mornings when it seems that the flick of a finger might make the whole sky ring. Below me, over the water, there is a sudden whir of flight, as a flock of ducks hurtles upstream. A little distance behind them, a pair of blatting, snake-necked geese sweeps smoothly past. White gulls, their bodies held aloft on supple wings, dance in the morning light.

I settle myself on the cool grass; it could be a long wait. Peregrines are not easy to see, a Cree elder named Stan Cuthand has warned me. "It's part of what makes them special. Peregrines are mystic birds."

My binoculars swing back to the rooftop and up the tallest spire. "They go to the heights," Cuthand had said, so high that people used to think they nested on the clouds. And the way they can shoot down out of nowhere to catch other birds in the air—just fold back their wings and plummet headfirst—is a wonder. "Fantastic birds," he called them. You can never tell quite when or where they will appear.

Peregrines have been living here, on the bank of the South Saskatchewan River, for the last two summers. They now nest right in the heart of the city of Saskatoon, where they lay their eggs on window ledges and hunt pigeons from the rooftops of the high-rise towers. This is my first season close to a peregrine nest. Finally, after hours of reading and talking about them, I will have a chance to watch them fly. People say they are the fastest birds in the world—the cheetahs of the sky. Perhaps I'll be able to see for myself why they, like few other creatures, seem always to have exercised a special power over the human mind.

My fingers are already chilled and stiff on the focussing knob. Have the falcons flown off to hunt, or are they just hidden from sight? Maybe they're perched under a ledge or behind a gargoyle; maybe, right now, they're glaring down at me with their eight-power eyes. What do they make of me, staring back with my eight-power binoculars? What, for that matter, do they make of the whole urban scene that spreads out around them?

The Saskatoon falcons are one of only about 15,000 breeding pairs in the world, a total that puts the peregrine among the rarest of birds. It is also one of the most widely distributed species on Earth, with nests on the sea crags and cliff-sides of six continents. Our pair numbers among the small but growing group of pioneers that nest in urban sites—on cathedrals and castles in Germany; on skyscrapers in Los Angeles, New York, Calgary, Montreal and two dozen other cities in North America. Like most of these city-dwellers, the pair in Saskatoon became established with the help of humankind, as part of a worldwide effort that began in the early 1970s, when the peregrine seemed doomed to extinction from the effects of pesticides.

In an attempt to augment the failing population, biologists in several countries bred falcons in captivity and released them to the wild. Saskatoon's male was hatched at the local univer-sity and turned loose from the roof of the Bessborough. The next spring, he made headlines in the local press by coming back to claim a territory. But scientists can't take credit for finding him a mate—she arrived of her own accord. She likely came from somewhere in the northern wilderness, but no one is sure. Neither can anyone explain why she showed up at just the right time to join the captive-reared male. How did she know the male was here, and why did she choose to settle above the asphalt and neon lights?

I pull my coat closer around me and study the skyline again, this time panning slowly to the south. A squat form perched on the corner of an office tower takes off in a haze of motion, then soars on backswept wings. Watch out, pigeon. Those falcons would love to capture you.

But what is this? On the roof of the neighbouring tower, twenty-five stories high, there is a tall antenna and, on top of that, spotlit by the sun, sits a bird. I focus frantically. Yes, dark head, light bib and chest, sleek contours, a little larger than a crow. Lazily, the bird stretches out one very long, sharp-pointed wing, slightly crooked at the "wrist." It must be—a peregrine.

So let the show begin! Fly for me, since that's your specialty. I remember the spectacular courtship displays I have read about, especially a report by Joseph A. Hagar that I'd found in an old bird book, *Life Histories of North American Birds of Prey*:

> Again and again the [male Peregrine] . . . started well to leeward and came along the cliff against the wind, diving, plunging, saw-toothing, rolling over and over, darting hither and yon like an autumn leaf until finally he would swoop up into the full current of air and be borne off on

To the ancient Egyptians, falcons were sacred birds and were sometimes mummified, as important people were.
HORST NIESTERS

the gale to do it all over again. At length he tired of this, and, soaring in narrow circles without any movement of his wings other than a constant small adjustment of their planes, he rose to a position 500 or 600 feet above the mountain and north of the cliff. Nosing over suddenly, he flicked his wings rapidly 15 or 20 times and fell like a thunderbolt. Wings half closed now, he shot down past the north end of the cliff, described three successive vertical loop-the-loops across its face, turning completely upside down at the top of each loop, and roared out over our heads with the wind rushing through his wings like ripping canvas. . . . The sheer excitement of watching such a performance was tremendous; we felt a strong impulse to stand and cheer.

How I'd love to see something like that! But the sun-warmed falcon on the rooftop doesn't want my applause. After a few minutes, it launches itself easily into the sky and soars in an unhurried arc around the building. Then, cutting the air briskly with strong, quick strokes, it heads upstream. I squint through the binoculars, straining to follow, but within seconds the bird is a speck and the speck is lost from sight.

So that's that: I have seen a peregrine. For this I have crawled out of bed at the crack of dawn and waxed poetic in the cold and damp? For this hundreds of people have filled thousands of pages with observations and data? This is the bird that has inspired a multimillion dollar recovery program? What is all the fuss about?

Yet quick on the heels of disappointment comes a rush of delight. As I walk home through the quiet streets, I realize that something has changed in me, not so much through glimpsing the peregrine as through the simple act of watching for it. It is as if I, and not just the morning, have now been filled with fresh clear light. To be out-of-doors at sunrise with every sense alert, attuned to the slightest movement, to the cut of every wing. To hear the bird song from the bushes, the woodpecker drumming on a nearby stump—that in itself has been worth something. It has shaken me out of the numbness of my everyday consciousness.

Sitting and waiting, with the river at my feet, I have known what it means to be alive and part of a living world. Is this what peregrine watchers have always been shown? I suddenly think of something else that Stan Cuthand said. Peregrines are messengers, he told me. They bring guidance from the Great Spirit, who was here before the world began and reveals itself to people through the creatures of this world. "Peregrines are mystic birds." Was this what he had meant?

A few days later, another adventure unfolds, but this time there is no need for patience or binoculars. A female peregrine is perched just behind me, in the cargo hold of Paddy Thompson's van. Like the male on the riverbank, this peregrine was bred in the falcon barn at the University of Saskatchewan and released to the wild, but, in an unusual intervention, she was recaptured in the fall. The idea was to safeguard her from the perils of the first winter journey, on which more than half of the young birds are lost. Now safely into her second spring, she is to be "flown" as a falconry bird for a few weeks to make sure that she is strong and skilled before she sets out on her own.

She is so close that I could touch her mottled breast with an outstretched hand. But I draw back: she already has enough to bear. Her head

The Egyptian falcon god Horus makes a gesture of purification or blessing. Horus imparted royal power to the pharaohs, who were worshipped as the incarnation of his deity. MUSÉE DU LOUVRE, PARIS

is encased in a leather hood, so that she cannot see; yet her neck flicks through a ninety-degree arch, left shoulder to centre, right shoulder to centre, over and over, as if she were doing her blind best to figure out where we are taking her. When the van swerves, her knobby toes grip the perch and her body works for balance.

"What would happen if you took the hood off?" I call to Paddy, who is in the front seat. He is a falcon breeder, researcher and falconer.

"She'd thrash around. Go crazy."

Okay, so it is better like this. The hood may be uncomfortable and it may look crude, but it is not cruel. In the case of the peregrine, I remind myself, the real cruelty had looked more ordinary. It had been wrapped up with the produce in our grocery stores and woven into the cotton clothing in our dresser drawers. The real harm had been done by twenty years' use of DDT and other pesticides to grow food and fibre crops. This subtle cruelty had almost caused the peregrine to disappear.

The falcon startles at a sound, freezes for a moment, then resumes the mechanical scan with her head. We round a corner, heading out of the city now, and her slender body sways against the turn. Since female peregrines are a third to a half larger than the males, I know that she's a good-sized creature, as falcons go. About the height of my forearm, I'd say, perhaps slightly less. But she looks very small, sitting there on her perch alone. Why, I wonder again, have people been moved to go to such lengths on behalf of her and her kind?

Around us, the stubbled hills shine in the long evening light. We drive south, west, south again. The ponds are dry; there has been an extended drought in this part of the world. The populations of ducks are very low, even lower than the dry years would lead one to expect. Finally, Paddy sees what he is looking for: a slough with a flock of waterfowl.

He lets his black Lab dog out of the back of the truck, then reaches with a gloved hand for the bird and nudges at her legs so that she will hop on board. Working with his teeth and his free hand, he pulls the hood from her face.

Without a moment's pause, the falcon leaps from his hand. Her wings pump hard against the air, and she heads up and away, sweeping wide circles over the crowns of the trees, and then (just because she can?) swoops down and skims close to the ground. She zooms by us, no higher than our knees; then, without so much as a beat of her wings, veers up and rides the sky again. In an instant, she is looking down on us and the treetops and everything.

Airborne, she is suddenly immense. She commands attention; she will be watched; she is everywhere. She belongs to the air. I am reminded of Hagar's notes: "an impulse to stand and cheer."

The ducks on the pond are silent. But as the falcon scoots off to the west, a reckless shoveller rises abruptly from the reeds and churns eastward. The falcon turns after it in a headstrong, wild-winged chase, but the duck is too far ahead, so she wheels and drops back towards the water. By now, the black dog has frightened another duck into flight, and this time there is no escape as the falcon swoops and swerves, making tight, last-minute turns, down for the kill. There is a bright splash as the duck hits the pond. Then all is still.

The next thing I know, the falcon is standing in tall grass at the edge of the pond. She stands over the duck, one foot wrapped grimly around its upper body; her head dips as she bites insistently at its neck. Bones crunch. She dips her beak down again and comes up with a mouthful of meat. Flurries of feathers drift past us as she plucks at the duck's breast.

She seems intent on feeding, but when the falconer "chucks" at her and offers his glove, she willingly hops on and sets to work on the dead quail he is gripping in his fist. She is a tame bird and—except for the memory of wings—commonplace once again. With a deft movement, the falconer slips the leather hood over her eyes.

But those wings . . .

When people moved up the valley of the Nile 5000 years ago, they brought a falcon god. Egyptologists say this god, who became known as Heru, or Horus—"that which is above," the Distant One—was inspired by the peregrine. The moment he was born, the old texts say, he took to the air. He soared "up into the sky, beyond the flight of the original bird-soul, beyond the stars . . . and all the divinities of olden time whose souls inhabit the constellations. He seemed to fly out into the vast regions beyond the limits of the divinely created universe and alighted upon the ramparts of the eastern horizon, the boundary of the world. In so doing he brought back light and the assurance of a new day."

A small group of robed forms stands at the base of a Nile cliff, their eyes turned towards a prehistoric dawn. Above the steep rock, a peregrine swoops and turns and dives; below, the faces of the watchers flicker with delight. Their braceleted arms reach out; they turn to each other and talk excitedly in a language we cannot understand; yet we are sure we catch the gist of it. "Did you see that? Fantastic birds! How do they do it?"

A rich fabric of myth and imagery was woven around the Egyptian falcon god. Here, he sits enthroned as the god of the sun and the son of the goddess Isis. Above him is a representation of his eyes, which were a powerful symbol in Egyptian magic. MUSÉE DU LOUVRE, PARIS

A group of falconers in the Persian Gulf state of Qatar prepare for a day's hunting. DR. FARIS AL-TIMIMI

Back in Paddy's yard, the well-fed peregrine has been put into her enclosure. I peer through the screened window, and she stares me straight in the face, fixing me with a dark, unwavering glare. For the Egyptians, the eye of Horus, the peregrine's eye, was a powerful symbol that signified wholeness and brought prophetic dreams.

In the earliest hieroglyphics, a falcon on a perch was a sign for "god." At the beginning of time, the Egyptians said, chaos reigned and silent waters covered the Earth, until some unknown being picked up a stick and stuck it into the soil of a small island. Immediately, a falcon swooped in out of the darkness and lit on the perch. The world suddenly became bright and the waters fell back to reveal land. When people appeared, they built a temple around the falcon to protect it. Sacred falcons that were housed and honoured at the temple of Horus at Edfu,

where these stories are still recorded on the walls, were mummified like the Pharoahs and interred in sacred cemeteries.

The falcon was a sky god and companion of the sun. Observing that the birds were often on the wing before sunrise (they are, in fact, most active at dawn and dusk), the Egyptians concluded that these vigorous creatures actually drew the sun into the new day and even turned the wheel of the year. "The sun goes around according to his purpose," says an ancient hymn to the falcon god. By association with this day-by-day act of renewal, the falcon became a symbol of transformation, rebirth and eternal life. Its emblem, a solar disk equipped with those familiar pointed wings, meant simply "to become."

But there was also a more practical side to ancient peoples' fascination with falcons. Peregrines are superb hunters that specialize in taking birds in midflight. Fast, adroit and fearless, they drop like missiles onto prey passing below and, in this way, are able to take species of birds many times their own size. While they have a special taste for pigeons, their menu generally reads like a field guide to the small- and medium-sized birds of the locality. Peregrines' spectacular proficiency at this challenging mode of life made them the awe and envy of human hunters for millenia, not just in Egypt but throughout the ancient world.

Yet once in human hands, these audacious predators are strangely docile, so it is not surprising that peregrines were among the first creatures to be tamed and put to work. "Falconry," the use of trained hawks and falcons to hunt for their keepers, is a discipline of great antiquity. As early as 750 B.C., Sumerian artists were chiselling out images of their emperor, Sargan the Great, riding out with his hawks. When Marco Polo journeyed to the Orient and, later, when the Crusaders rampaged through the Middle East, they encountered a richly developed practice of falconry that was already centuries old. In western Europe, the sport reached its height in the Middle Ages, when it was assimilated to the intricacies of feudal life. Peregrines were classed amongst the "noble hawks" and reserved for the upper reaches of society.

As Roger Tory Peterson put it in *Birds over America*, the "dispassionate brown eyes" of the peregrine, more than those of any other bird, were "witness to the struggle for civilization, from the squalid tents on the steppes of Asia thousands of years ago, to the marble halls of European Kings in the seventeenth century."

But the invention of guns shattered this intimacy, and a dark age in the relationship between peregrines and people began. No longer the allies of human hunters, the birds suddenly were seen as competitors and enemies. By the eighteenth century, falcons, hawks and eagles were being systematically slaughtered across western Europe, usually under the inducement of official rewards. In 1718, for example, King Frederick William I of Prussia decreed that predatory animals and birds were to be eradicated—not just controlled, but wiped out—in order to protect hares and grouse for sport hunting. Year after year, thousands of raptors were killed. In the little kingdom of Hanover in 1776–77, officials amassed a grisly heap of 14,125 pairs of talons, turned in for bounty. Thirty years later, a Scottish marquess proposed an oath for British gamekeepers that ended with the chilling words: ". . . and finally I shall use my best endeavours to destroy all birds of prey, etc., with their nests, etc. wherever they can be found therein. So help me God."

Meanwhile, as Europeans journeyed out into new worlds (with that same confidence in divine sponsorship), the carnage spread to other continents. For 250 years, there was no looking back. As late as the 1960s, about 120,000 birds of prey were being destroyed each year in the Soviet Union; perhaps half that number were being netted on their migration routes in France and either stamped to death or plucked alive *pour rigoler* (for a laugh). Writing in 1974, biologist Maarten Bijleveld charged that in "the past fifteen to twenty years at least several million birds of prey were destroyed in Europe alone. The responsibility for this state of affairs can be assigned almost exclusively to . . . hunters, who still today continue to perpetrate this destruction in many countries and for what they consider to be their own interest." He could have made a similar case for Canada, the United States and many other parts of the "civilized" world.

The destruction of falcons and other birds of prey has now been curtailed (though not eliminated) by law and public education. And happily, the campaign of extinction, for all its brutality, was never particularly successful against peregrines. Through the centuries of persecution, the number of breeding peregrines showed little change in most regions. Even with additional harassment from egg collectors, some of whom had an insatiable greed for the peregrines' beautifully marked shells, the nest-cliffs generally remained full year after year. Similarly, falconers who took chicks or juveniles from the wild seem to have had little effect on the population in most areas.

Not even the firepower of the British air force could beat the birds back for long. During the Second World War, the RAF killed peregrines along certain stretches of the British coast in order to protect pigeons that carried messages from U-boat patrols. In the short term, this operation was successful, but as soon as the war was over, the unstoppable peregrines returned to their cliffs.

Yet, fifteen years later, these and thousands of other peregrine nest sites were empty, and no one had a clue why the birds had disappeared. In fact, for the longest time, nobody even noticed that they were missing. If peregrines were still speaking on behalf of eternity, it seemed for the moment that no one was listening.

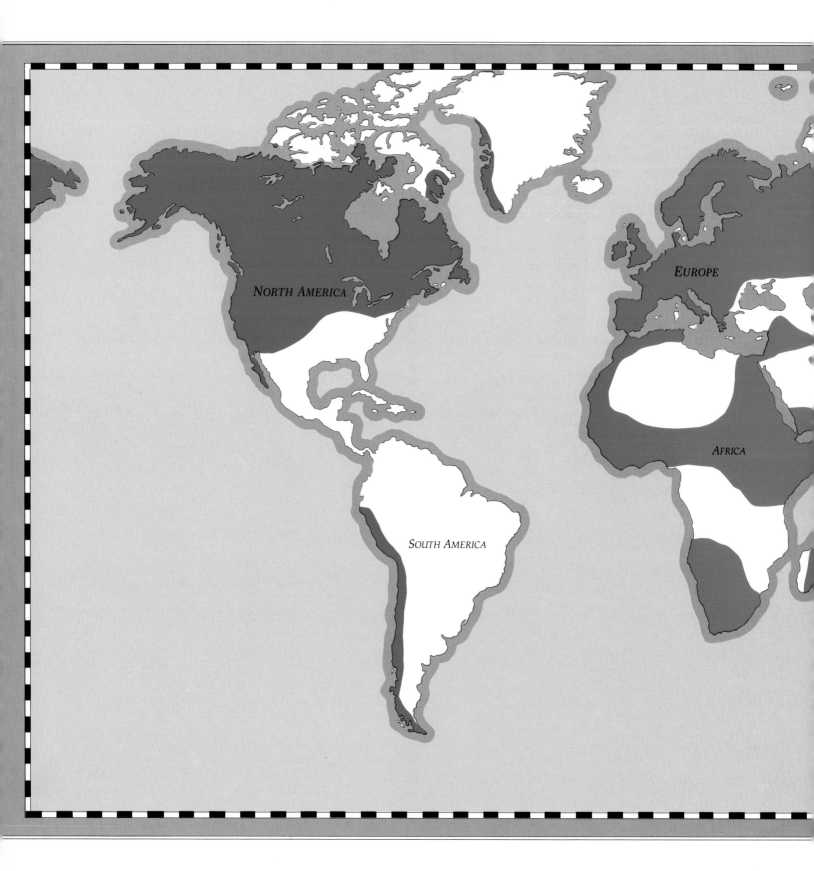

NORTH AMERICA

SOUTH AMERICA

EUROPE

AFRICA

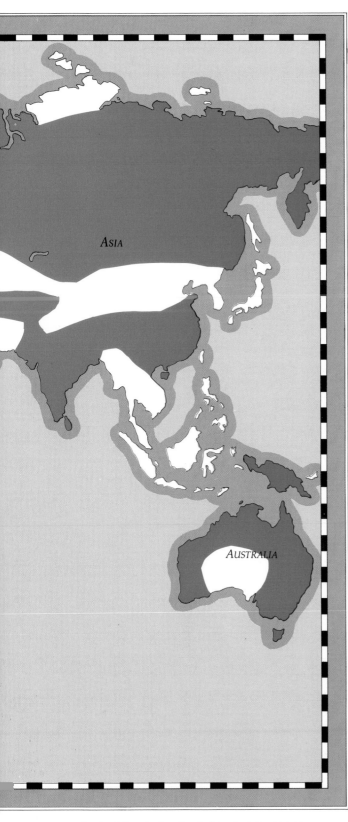

GLOBAL DISTRIBUTION OF THE

PEREGRINE FALCON

ASIA

AUSTRALIA

Based on information from *Peregrine Falcon Populations: Their Management and Recovery* by T. J. Cade et al. (The Peregrine Fund Inc., 1988)

Today, as for thousands of years, the peregrine helps us to feel our connections with the living Earth. Here, a young peregrine stands against the landscape of the Colorado Plateau in the southwestern United States, a region in which falcons continued to nest during the declines of recent decades. Lamentably, the species is still threatened or endangered in many parts of North America and Europe. DAVID H. ELLIS; *INSET:* FRANS LANTING/MINDEN PICTURES

A peregrine falcon shelters its downy brood on a cliff-side nest in the Canadian Arctic. "Everyone adores the falcon's beauty," the ancient Egyptians said. MARK BRADLEY

Peregrines inhabit some of the wildest and least accessible terrain on Earth. A remarkably adaptable species, they are among the most widely distributed of birds, with nests on every continent except Antarctica. Perhaps that is why they earned the name of Falco peregrinus, *the "wandering falcon." Wherever they range, peregrines usually seek out sheer rock walls, like the one shown here, on which to raise their families.* DAVID H. ELLIS

This youngster is about a month old. Note the long, slender toes with black claws. Adult peregrines use their feet to strike and grab prey as they pursue it through the air. DAVID H. ELLIS

In northern and western Finland, peregrines have adopted an unusual mode of life. Faced with a landscape that lacks cliffs, they have learned to nest on the ground in the middle of large bogs. Although this countryside looks very different from the peregrine's regular habitat, the bogs resemble the nesting cliffs in one important way. Both provide protection from land predators.

Above: A peregrine lounges in the sunshine, overlooking its bog. Right: A falcon breaks its flight as it plunges into the shrubbery. Perhaps it is grabbing for a small bird or, less likely, a rodent. JORMA LUHTA

With its dark, keen-eyed stare and the metallic sheen of its beak, the peregrine creates an impression of power—and so it should. Peregrines catch birds in flight, a livelihood that calls for intelligence, agility, speed and a fiery spirit. Other adaptations for the chase include the toothlike notch on the bill, which is used to kill prey, and the structure in the centre of the nostril, which may serve as a baffle to deflect the rush of air so the bird can breathe during a headlong descent. STEVE KAUFMAN

Sometimes, though it's by no means common, peregrines live in forests and nest in trees. Tree-dwelling populations have now been discovered in Sweden, Australia, Alaska and the northwestern United States. Tragically, the tree-nesters of central Europe, which flourished before the introduction of DDT and other pesticides, are now extinct.
ART WOLFE

Above and bottom left: *Just as wolves and humans are built for the chase on the ground, so peregrines are designed for pursuit through the air. Or, to make the comparison more dynamic, they are the dolphins of the sky, sinuous and zestful in flight. Their long, sharp-cut wings are shaped for speed and free-flowing turns.* ABOVE: © WAYNE LYNCH; *BOTTOM LEFT:* JON TRIFFO

Left: *Wherever they choose to nest—on the ground, in trees or on cliffs—peregrines crave access to open country and, especially, open skies. This peregrine stands against the brilliant air of Bodmin Moor in Cornwall, England.* ANDY ROUSE

Safe nest sites, big skies and an abundance of food make the world complete for a peregrine. In the background, a flock of western sandpipers (one of many species on which peregrines prey) flies up in alarm, while in the foreground a successful hunter prepares for a meal. ADRIAN DORST; *FOREGROUND:* ART WOLFE

A young hunter wheels away from its handler's gloved fist. Because of their spectacular speed, fearless nature and hunting skill, peregrines have long been a favourite of falconers.

Although some people object to falconry as a blood sport, it is worth remembering that falconers were at the heart of efforts to rescue the peregrine in several countries, including Germany, Canada and the United States. Not only did they care passionately about the survival of "their" birds, but they also contributed essential knowledge and skills—

where to find nests, how to live-trap wild birds, how to raise them in captivity and so on. As a case in point, this young falcon is a research subject that has been captured, banded and released, using techniques first developed by falconers.
THOMAS L. MAECHTLE

Peregrines are about the size and weight of a large crow, yet they can kill birds of a much larger size, such as this fat duck. In tribute to their ability as duck hunters, North American peregrines used to be known as "duck hawks."
STEVE KAUFMAN

Left: *Peregrines have a varied repertoire of hunting strategies. Sometimes they chase after their prey like the falcon shown here, which is closing on a pigeon, probably at a speed of about 100 k.p.h. (60 m.p.h.).*

Peregrines that live on the coast often fly out over the ocean to hunt. They skim along at high speed, following the contour of the waves, and use the crests as cover to take sea birds by surprise. Sometimes they employ the same technique over the tops of dense forests.

Their most celebrated exploit is the "stoop," in which they leap off a high perch or mount up into the sky, then fold their wings and dash headfirst towards their prey hundreds of metres below. They have been clocked at speeds of up to 470 k.p.h. (270 m.p.h.). On contact, they often daze their prey and send it tumbling groundward, then swoop down to catch it in their talons and deliver a killing bite while still in flight. DENVER BRYAN

Right: *A peregrine plucks a mallard duck. Note the falconer's jess (a short strap that attaches to a leash) on its right leg.* STEVE KAUFMAN

Bottom right: *A peregrine spreads its wings and "cacks" as it defends a ring-necked pheasant that it has killed.* ALAN AND SANDY CAREY

Like many other predators, peregrines are able to gobble down huge amounts of meat in one sitting. In fact, they have been known to eat a quarter or more of their own weight in a single meal. (To put this in human terms, imagine an average-sized woman who could eat 130 hamburger patties in one sitting.) Peregrines also cache food in the nooks and crannies of their nest-cliffs and return to it, days later, when they need a snack. ABOVE: DAVID H. ELLIS; *RIGHT:* FRANS LANTING/MINDEN PICTURES

Perhaps because of their gory diet, peregrines take special delight in bathing. In addition to nest sites, open spaces and plenty to eat, their chosen habitat usually includes enough water for frequent baths. MICHAEL S. QUINTON

Their hunger satisfied, two young falcons settle in for a drowsy morning on their hunting grounds. It seems incongruous that these peaceful-looking creatures should have been caught up in an ecological horror story.
JORMA LUHTA

A falcon flies off with a full load in its rounded crop. An adult male peregrine needs a bird the size of a cuckoo (about 100 grams or 3.5 ounces) each day. A female, being larger, needs something on the order of a jay (150 grams or 5 ounces).

Like people, peregrines are at the top of their food chain or, to make the image more accurate, they are at the apex of a food pyramid. This means that nutrients flow to them from the whole ecosystem in which they live: from the soil or sea, on to plants or plankton, insects or fish, land birds or sea birds, and then to peregrines. Unfortunately, so-called "persistent" pesticides (those that are not readily digested or broken down) can travel freely through the same far-reaching networks. In fact, they may accumulate as they move up, putting the peregrine and other top-level creatures at special risk.
JON TRIFFO

THE DDT CRISIS

It was a strange beginning for a mystery. A Welsh pigeon keeper named Ivor George went on TV one day in 1960 with an urgent request: the law against killing peregrine falcons must immediately be revoked. Pigeon fanciers needed the right to combat their traditional enemy, he argued, especially at a time when the population of these rapacious, tooth-beaked killers was on a sudden rise. Unprecedented numbers of homing pigeons—expensive, highly bred birds—were being slaughtered, he cried, and the pigeon fanciers were unable to come to their defence.

A petition was launched, pressing the same demands, and the British Home Office, with what must have seemed to the signers to be ponderous thoroughness, launched an enquiry. The task of assessing the situation was assigned to Derek Ratcliffe, a professional biologist and an amateur peregrine enthusiast. Ever since boyhood and his first exhilarating scrambles over a peregrine cliff, he had had "the fever," as he called it. Despite the ominous context of his investigation, he was delighted at the chance to study these "marvellous" birds for a couple of years and even get paid for it.

The charges put forward by the pigeon fanciers raised two issues. In the first place, "the fancy" contended that peregrines eat pigeons. Of this, neither Ratcliffe nor any other serious peregrine watcher could entertain much doubt. Early in his career, for example, Ratcliffe had clambered into an aerie "in which three fine eyasses [chicks] glared out from amidst a gory shambles of pigeon remains"; and over the years he had often collected empty rings, or bands, from homers when he visited peregrine nests. Given that a typical peregrine family—mother, father and two or three young—eats about 225 kilograms (about 500 pounds) of bird flesh in a year and that many pairs show a special fondness for domestic pigeons, Ratcliffe thought that the fanciers' suspicions might well be legitimate.

But the other aspect of their case was less obvious. Was it really true that peregrines were increasing in number, as the pigeon keepers said? One of the most striking characteristics of British peregrines had always been their exceptional constancy. Writing in the twelfth century, one Giraldus Cambrensis had commented on the "remarkable fact [that] in the history of this tribe of birds, . . . their nests are not more numerous than they were many centuries ago; and although they have broods every year, their numbers do not increase." Until the pigeon-keepers' protest, the British population was assumed to have remained stable, at about 800 pairs, since at least the time of Queen Elizabeth I. What's more, it had also long been noted that the falcons tended to use the same nest-cliffs that had been favoured by their distant ancestors. There were, for example, written records to prove that an island off the coast of Wales had been occupied by peregrines since 1243 A.D.

Could it be true that the British peregrines had now undergone an unprecedented upsurge? Might they be overflowing into new habitat? To answer these questions, Ratcliffe first made a catalogue of peregrine nest sites by gathering reports from the ornithological literature and putting out a call to bird watchers, falconers, egg collectors and others. He determined that, in

any given year, more than four-fifths of the cliffs on his list were generally in use. Thus prepared, he set out with high anticipation to count peregrines on their nests.

What he discovered was dismaying in every respect. Instead of tightly spaced territories and ledges crowded with young, he often found—nothing. Far too often, the peregrine cliffs were bare: in the south of England, only 8 per cent of nest sites were occupied. "The once flourishing population of southern England had all but disappeared," he later wrote, ". . . and over the country as a whole a large number of nesting places once held regularly by Peregrines seemed to be totally deserted, in many cases for the first time ever known." The falcons that remained had few young or none at all; some had not even laid eggs. The survey also confirmed an inexplicable observation that Ratcliffe had first made in 1951 and had noted all too often in the intervening decade. Where breeding birds remained, many of their nests contained fragments of broken egg shell. Since the early 1950s, he and other observers had also noted a perverse new behaviour among the falcons: they had been known to eat their own eggs.

The survey results for 1962 were even worse than those of the year before: the zone of collapse seemed to be spreading rapidly north. In the country as a whole, the peregrine population had fallen past the halfway mark and seemed likely to approach zero within the next five years. Far from settling Mr. George's concerns, Ratcliffe had uncovered a sinister and unexpected pattern.

Meanwhile, on the other side of the Atlantic, the plot was about to take another discomfiting turn. It started innocently enough at a big international meeting of ornithologists held at

Cornell University. Among the delegates to the congress was a cheerful, even-tempered biologist from Wisconsin named Joseph Hickey. Everybody knew he was interested in peregrines—in the early 1940s, he had published a study of all known nest sites from the Rockies to the east coast—so somebody passed on the latest word. Rumour had it that, in 1962, no young peregrines had been fledged in the entire northeastern states.

Hickey was too good a scientist to be swayed by unsubstantiated and unlikely talk: "I think I assumed that falconers—real and would-be—had been very, very busy" stealing young from nests, he later recalled. Then, in 1963, came "the real shocker." Hickey learned about Derek Ratcliffe's research. Suddenly, the idle chitchat about breeding failure was transformed into a chilling hypothesis.

Twenty-two thousand, five hundred and twenty-six kilometres and 133 aeries later, Hickey and his assistants could confirm the worst. Every single nest site they visited had been deserted. Further research enlarged the catastrophe: the peregrine falcon had disappeared from the eastern third of North America—from the Atlantic coast to the Mississippi River and north to the boreal forest. Elsewhere on the continent, where the birds were still nesting, their numbers seemed greatly reduced in most areas, even in remote parts of Alaska and the Canadian North. By the mid-1970s, Hickey and his colleagues knew of only 648 breeding peregrines in an area that, thirty years earlier, was thought to have supported 18,000 nests.

Soon similar horror stories were being told in Finland, Norway, Sweden, Denmark, Belgium, France, Poland and the Baltic states. In Germany a population of 900 had dwindled to 90, and a rare group of tree-nesting peregrines had become extinct. Eventually, population declines of greater or less magnitude would be reported in at least thirty-six countries on five continents, from the Soviet Union (now the Commonwealth of Independent States) to Australia and Canada to Japan.

Almost as shocking as the declines themselves was the fact that they had gone largely unnoticed. A favourite species had been eradicated from large parts of Europe and North America, and the public had not known about it. If it hadn't been for the eccentric demands of the pigeon keepers, the peregrine could have vanished from Earth before anyone raised the alarm. And even after the problem had been perceived, the cause remained distressingly obscure. The situation was totally abnormal—nothing of the sort had ever been known to happen before—and none of the common-sense explanations seemed worth considering. Human persecution? A new disease? It seemed unlikely that either could strike on such a large scale and with such furtive speed.

There was another possible angle on the case, though it too seemed far-fetched. Could it be that the new generation of postwar pesticides was somehow implicated in the peregrine's disappearance? The evidence for this suspicion was solely circumstantial. For one thing, the timing looked right. Though no one knew exactly when the peregrine crash had begun, it could not have been before the early 1940s, when Hickey had documented a flourishing population in the eastern U.S. As it happened, the early forties was exactly when the Allied armies had developed the first of the "organochlorine" family of synthetic insecticides, a compound that went by the nickname of DDT. "When war was imminent," American authors J. C. Leary, W. I. Fishbein and L. C. Salter wrote,

> the public's cry was all for ships, tanks, and planes for the defense of America. But in the secret councils of the men whose duty it was to plan and lead, the prayer was for ships, planes, tanks—and a truly good insecticide!... [T]hey knew that if they lost the first battle to disease they stood a good chance of losing to their human enemies as well, for a sick soldier cannot fight and typhus or yellow fever can kill fighting men in greater numbers than bullets....
>
> DDT proved to be the answer, a weapon as potent against disease-carrying insects as the B29s and P80s and the atomic bomb were against Germany and Japan.

"The research effort poured into DDT is on the scale of the $2,000,000,000 expended on the atomic bomb," the same authors reported. And it seemed well worth the expense: from the beginning, the compound seemed destined "to take a place as the best weapon yet discovered in man's ages-long war with a hitherto unconquerable enemy, the insects." This chemical superhero was released for civilian use in 1945 and within two years was being applied on a massive scale.

In many ways, DDT seemed an ideal insecticide. It was effective against a wide range of pests, including those that attacked forests and farms. It was chemically stable and long-lasting, so that, once applied, it went on working for months or years. And it seemed entirely safe for use around people. In one of its first applications, almost the entire citizenry of Naples had been doused with DDT powder to ward off

an outbreak of typhus. As the compound came into general use, North American children played in the spray from trucks that fogged their neighbourhoods. Yet nobody showed any ill effects from this direct exposure. Indeed, DDT did not seem very toxic to any warm-blooded creatures, whether people or peregrines.

At the same time, it was obvious that the impact of DDT on birds and wildlife, at least, had not been carefully researched. "The Army has not been interested in that phase," a DDT proponent confessed with easy candour, in a tract entitled "DDT and the Insect Problem." "The military purpose was to kill mosquitoes and lice, to protect the lives of soldiers and keep them on the fighting line, no matter what happened to the fish, the Japs, the birds, or any other accidental victim." Similarly, in the peacetime battle against starvation and pestilence (or in the scramble to maximize profits), weak-kneed misgivings about possible harm to humans or wildlife could not be allowed to delay the victory. Besides, the few studies that had been carried out, like those in which chickens and songbird nests were treated with DDT, did not point to any problems.

But there were two other insect poisons, younger cousins of DDT, which had a much harder time maintaining their knight-in-shining-armour glow of innocence. Aldrin and dieldrin were second-generation organochlorine compounds introduced in 1956 and widely used, especially in Britain, as seed dressings. This meant that the insecticides were applied to seed grains, which were then sown over the countryside. Unfortunately, the poisoned seeds were both highly attractive and highly toxic to seed-eating birds (including homing pigeons, perhaps?). Almost as soon as the new chemicals were introduced, British naturalists began reporting catastrophic die-offs of wild birds, not only seed eaters but also bird eaters such as sparrowhawks and kestrels.

Like DDT, aldrin and dieldrin were highly stable compounds that retained their full power to kill even after being eaten by a seed eater. Like DDT too, they were fat-soluble. If seed eaters took in small amounts of poison over a period of time, they might escape death themselves, but their fat would become contaminated with increasing amounts of insecticide. The poisons were then passed on, in large and often lethal doses, from the seed eaters to their predators, which went into fatal convulsions or literally dropped dead in flight.

Was this what was happening to the peregrines? The timing was certainly plausible—in Britain, at any rate, the falcons had taken a nose-dive the very year after aldrin and dieldrin came into use—and so was the geography. In Britain again, for example, peregrines had fared worst in the south, where agricultural chemicals were used most heavily. But if this theory was correct, then why were the falcons of non-agricultural areas such as Finland, Greenland, the Yukon and Alaska also in big trouble? And what could account for the low number of nestlings and the mysterious broken shells? If aldrin and dieldrin turned out to be the main culprits, was DDT an accomplice? What about all the other members of the organochlorine gang—heptachlor, HCH, lindane, toxaphene and industrial PCBs—that had been turned loose on the countryside in the late 1940s and the 1950s?

When a mass killer is on the loose, a good detective follows all leads, however vague they may seem. The British investigator Derek Ratcliffe was a good detective. First, he was able to

show that infertile eggs from more than a dozen aeries, including some that were far from farm country, all contained trace amounts of dieldrin, DDE (the main breakdown product of DDT) and other pesticides. Then a falcon that died at its nest in Devon was shown to have ingested a similar poison broth—its liver was laced with dieldrin, DDE and other compounds in quantities that, together, constituted a lethal dose.

But the clincher for Ratcliffe's case came in the late 1960s. Because of public protests about the deaths of seed eaters and raptors, the use of aldrin and dieldrin was restricted in Britain in 1962 and again in 1964. Almost immediately, the peregrine population stabilized, and by 1967 the resilient falcons were actually on the upsurge. Again, the evidence was circumstantial, but for Ratcliffe and many others, it was good enough. Peregrines had declined, at least in part and at least in Great Britain, because they had been "accidental victims" of aldrin and dieldrin, which had accumulated in their prey and killed the adult falcons. Dead birds can't produce young, and so the species had begun to disappear.

But was this the whole story? It was disquieting to remember that the surviving birds (the ones that had avoided outright poisoning) weren't having much luck producing young either. Clutches continued to be small; eggshells were fragile, and some adults were still eating their own embryos. Ratcliffe's data showed that these problems had first appeared at least five years *before* aldrin and dieldrin came into use. Curiously, this was just at the time when DDT and a similar compound called lindane were introduced. "I was led to wonder," Ratcliffe recalled, "if this phenomenon could be a response to one or other of these less toxic [that is, lethal]

In eastern Germany, peregrine eggs still showed severe DDT *damage in the late 1980s.* DR. GERT KLEINSTÄUBER

pesticides." What if, for example, these chemicals caused peregrine eggshells to become thin and breakable?

There was no obvious reason to think this might be so. What little was known about DDT suggested that it affected the liver and nerves, not the reproductive system. Still, *faute de mieux*, it was at least worth checking out. Spurred on by Joe Hickey and other colleagues, Ratcliffe quickly put his hunches to the test. First, he measured a sample of post-DDT shells; then he turned to the peregrines' erstwhile enemies, the egg collectors, for shells that dated from earlier decades.

> A tour of the country began, with my weighing machine and calipers, and the records grew rapidly as I went through those mahogany drawers with their cherished loot from the wild

places of Britain. There was soon no doubt at all that eggshells of the Peregrine taken after 1947 were very significantly thinner, by almost 20% over the country as a whole, than those taken before this year.

What's more, he found similar deterioration in the eggs of sparrowhawks, merlins, golden eagles and other raptors, all dating from the same time. In North America, scientists quickly extended Ratcliffe's research to include their own peregrine populations, plus bald eagles, brown pelicans and several other flesh- and fish-eating birds.

On both sides of the Atlantic, researchers took up the problem and were soon able to prove conclusively that DDT causes eggshell thinning. They also discovered a rough relationship between the amount of DDE in the egg and the fragility of the shell. What's more, DDT appeared to be responsible for other reproductive problems, such as small clutches and egg-eating. Obviously, aldrin and dieldrin were not the only villains.

"The greatest strength of birds as environmental monitors is that people care about them," pesticide expert David Peakall has aptly pointed out. From the beginning, it has been clear that a great many people care very deeply about peregrine falcons. Not only was the use of aldrin and dieldrin greatly curtailed, at least partly on the falcons' account, but DDT and other suspect organochlorines were restricted or outlawed in most European and North American countries by the early 1970s. And these bans were achieved despite a fierce fight from the chemical industry. The peregrine falcon provided the emotional and scientific heart of the anti-DDT campaign, particularly in Canada and the United States.

But "the plight of the peregrine"—the guilty image of the species' headlong fall; the mute fact of the hundreds of empty aeries—seemed to some to call for an even larger response. They dreamed of breeding peregrines in captivity and releasing them to the wild, in the hope of seeing them fly free over their cliffs again. Some people said flatly that it couldn't be done, but the first successes came in the early 1970s, thanks to the efforts of Heinz Meng, Tom J. Cade and others in the United States. Then in 1977 a peregrine bred by Richard Fyfe of the Canadian Wildlife Service made history by mating and raising young in the wild. Since then, more than 4000 captive-bred peregrines have been released in Canada and the United States, as well as smaller numbers in Sweden and Germany, and hun-

dreds of breeding pairs have become established. For example, the hundred-plus pairs that now nest in the eastern United States are all released birds or their progeny.

With or without human help, the peregrine is on the wing again throughout much of its range, in numbers that may soon approach natural levels. But it would be a mistake to take too much comfort from this happy ending. In particular, it would be foolish to conclude that we can go on making reckless errors in our use of synthetic poisons, as we did with the organochlorines, and get away scot-free.

To this day—after thirty years of intensive research—scientists still do not know which chemical was the main culprit in the peregrine's near-demise. Did the birds decline primarily because of direct poisoning by aldrin and dieldrin, which killed the breeding birds, or through the covert action of DDT, which permitted the breeding birds to live but prevented them from reproducing properly? While everyone now agrees that both processes were involved, British researchers place more stress on the former explanation and North Americans on the latter. A clear final verdict is still not in. Researchers are also uncertain about the role of other members of the organochlorine family, especially PCBs, which may someday have to take a share of the blame for the peregrines' suffering.

If we cannot answer these questions after the fact, when we know precisely which species have been harmed and in what way, how can we imagine ourselves capable of predicting the effects of new chemicals before they are introduced into the biosphere? Which of the thousands of species of insects, fish, amphibians, birds, mammals and plants may be affected?

A peregrine chick studies the alien world of the laboratory. Falcons raised in captivity helped to boost wild populations in several countries. FRANS LANTING/MINDEN PICTURES

Which life processes will be weakened? How will our new chemicals interact with the thousands of other novel toxins that we have already released into our soil, water and air? It is literally impossible to answer these questions before each new chemical is introduced. By continuing to rely heavily on pesticides and other synthetic compounds, we are conducting a desperate experiment on the biosphere and on ourselves.

Thirty years ago, just as the DDT crisis was breaking, Rachel Carson published her masterpiece, *Silent Spring*. In it, in exact and passionate prose, she argued that it is "impossible to predict the effects of lifetime exposure to chemical and physical agents that are not part of [our] biological experience." This is precisely the lesson of the peregrine crisis and one that we have yet to learn.

A "hack" box, where captive-bred falcon chicks can be fed and fledged, is installed on the face of a cliff.
R. WAYNE NELSON

PEREGRINE FALCONS:

IN THE DANGER ZONE

After the Second World War, many peregrine falcon populations around the world suffered a steep decline, and the species seemed on a headlong dive towards extinction. But when the use of DDT and other insecticides was restricted in the early 1970s, the resilient falcons surged ahead, and today they are back on their aeries in many parts of the world.

Unfortunately, this recovery has not been universal. Though it now seems unlikely that the peregrine will vanish from Earth, there are large regions in which the species' future is extremely uncertain. These include, in Europe: Hungary, Czechoslovakia, Poland, eastern Germany, Finland, Scandinavia and the sea coasts of southeast England; in North America: the Canadian prairies and the northern Rockies of the United States, plus central California, Oregon and Washington; and in Australia: the agricultural regions of the state of Victoria. Elsewhere—in Africa, the Middle East, the Soviet Union and Asia— the status of the peregrine is virtually unknown.

This chart shows the number of pairs of peregrines in various countries and regions at three times: before DDT was introduced, after the population crashed, and in the most recent year for which figures are available. The numbers shown are all approximate and are based on figures in Peregrine Falcon Populations: Their Management and Recovery *(The Peregrine Fund, Inc., 1988) and the results of the 1975 North American peregrine falcon survey* (Canadian Field-Naturalist 90: 228–73).

Before DDT (early 1940s)

After DDT (mid-1970s)

Present (late 1980s)

NORTH AMERICA

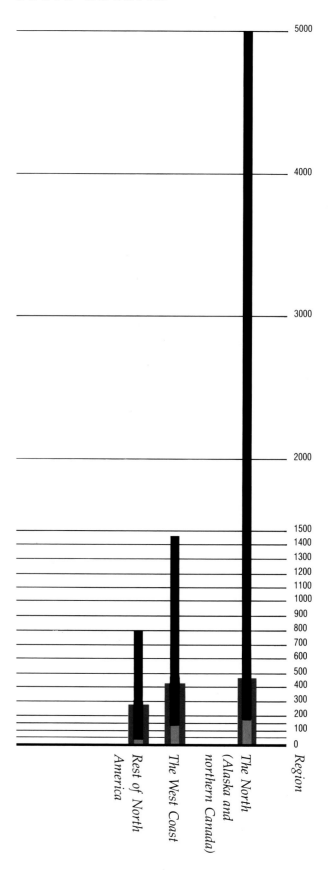

EUROPE

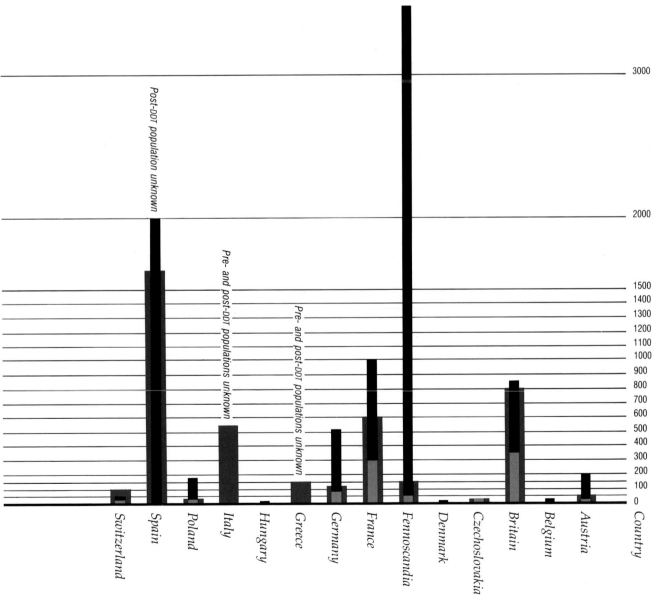

Above: *With the safety of the sky at its feet, a peregrine stands on the ramparts of its nest-cliff. Yet the natural defences of its habitat provide no protection against modern pollutants, such as the organochlorine family of insect poisons.* LAYNE KENNEDY

Fortunately, as soon as these insect poisons were restricted or withdrawn, peregrines were able to breed normally in many parts of the world. Left: *A clutch of healthy peregrine eggs. Peregrines ordinarily lay three or four eggs, sometimes as few as one and, rarely, as many as seven. About half the size of chicken eggs, they are a delicate cream or pink colour and are marked with red or rich brown.* HANNU HAUTALA

Peregrines do not build nests of their own, though sometimes they take over structures built by other birds, such as ravens, crows and hawks. In the northern hemisphere, they usually breed in late winter or early spring. ART WOLFE

Usually a falcon lays her eggs in a simple hollow, or scrape, on the face of a cliff. Although this behaviour may seem lackadaisical, peregrines are actually very particular about their nesting places. Of all the apparently suitable nooks and crannies in the rocks, falcons accept very few. Each pair may have two or three safe ledges on its territory, which they use in alternate years. Often these sites are occupied for many generations. Carbon-dating of remains at an Australian nest site showed that falcons had been using it for 19,000 years.

When the DDT crisis ended and peregrines returned to their nesting cliffs, often after a lapse of decades, they often laid their eggs in the very spots used by their ancestors. MARK BRADLEY

An adult peregrine falcon shows off its regal plumage. Since males and females exhibit the same elegant markings, there is no way to identify this bird by sex. Sometimes, however, it is possible to distinguish the sexes by size. Adult females, at weights of 850 grams (1.9 pounds) and up, look bigger and sturdier than the males, which can weigh less than 600 grams (1.25 pounds). MICHEL JULIEN/VALAN PHOTOS

Once the full clutch is laid, the female sits very closely over the nest. She will remain on duty, with only brief breaks, for the month-long incubation. The male, being smaller, may be less well suited to keep the eggs warm and usually is only permitted to cover the nest for brief periods. GORDON COURT

Left: *From the time the eggs begin to form in her body until the chicks are half-grown, the mother peregrine does very little hunting. But she doesn't lose her interest in the tantalizing array of small birds that flutter past. This nest-bound female cranes her neck to watch swallows swooping over her head.* RICHARD FYFE

Above: *The male, meanwhile, hunts for himself and his mate. Later, when the chicks hatch, he will bring in most of the food for the young family. Agile, light on his wings, he is especially good at catching small birds and usually has no problem in keeping the nest well provisioned.* KATHY WATKINS/IMAGES OF NATURE

Maybe this is why we call it "baby-sitting"! When the chicks are very small, one of the parents, usually the female, stays with the youngsters almost constantly. The chicks need protection against the extremes of early spring weather (heat, cold, rain, snow) and against predators, such as great horned or eagle owls.

Because many peregrines will temporarily abandon their nests if they are alarmed—leaving eggs or young exposed—anyone approaching an aerie must do so with great caution. Eggs and young chicks may die if they become chilled or overheated, so it is especially important to leave the birds alone during extreme weather. KATHY WATKINS/IMAGES OF NATURE

Dead chicks, swept out of the nest during a spring storm, lie in a heap at the foot of their nest-cliff. Though sad, this kind of natural loss does not usually harm the population as a whole. A pair of peregrines produces an average of one or two chicks each year, more than enough to make up for those that are lost through accident, predation and disease. But they may not be able to reproduce quickly enough to compensate for additional, unnatural losses, such as those caused by human disturbance or pollution. KATHY WATKINS/IMAGES OF NATURE

Rough and daring as hunters, peregrines are gentle with their young and feed them with extraordinary tenderness.
KATHY WATKINS/IMAGES OF NATURE

In the wide silence of the Canadian tundra, a male peregrine arrives to relieve the female at the nest. His head-down gesture may be meant to appease the female, who is generally dominant over her mate. KATHY WATKINS/IMAGES OF NATURE

A cuddlesome brood of peregrine chicks snoozes in the spring light. The pointed bumps near the tips of their beaks are "egg teeth," which were used to chip through the tough shell when they were hatching. RICHARD FYFE

This young falcon is moving out of its downy infancy and into the first stage of "childhood." Note the pinfeathers that are beginning to sprout on its wings, a change that begins when the youngster is about three weeks old. Falcon chicks thrust their claws out like this when they are frightened. GALEN ROWELL/MOUNTAIN LIGHT

This brood of wailing youngsters is quite prepared to take on the photographer, though they are only about three weeks old. SEPPO SAARI

Framed by spikes of fireweed, three peregrine chicks enjoy the security of an open bog in Finland. Young falcons often plop down on their "bums" with their legs stretched out in front of them, like the bird in the centre is doing.
SEPPO SAARI

Though still obviously a baby, this five-week-old falcon is beginning to show signs of the bird it will become.
RICHARD FYFE

Left: *Though it will be weeks before it can fly, much less hunt, this tiny peregrine chick is already taking an interest in passing birds.* RICHARD FYFE

A falcon chick stretches its long, unwieldy wings. Though the bird will not be able to fly for another two weeks, its outstretched wing is already shaped for speed and stunt-flying. RICHARD FYFE

Three half-grown peregrines stand contentedly amidst a litter of pigeon remains. By the time the chicks reach this stage, both the female parent and the male parent are hunting for their voracious nestlings. This brood was photographed in southern Scotland. R. MEARNS

Inset: *This well-fed youngster wears traces of its dinner on its face, and its purplish crop bulges through its feathers and down.* PETER LINDBERG

As long as they have plenty to eat, young falcons usually get along well with their siblings. They share food with each other, preen one another's feathers and play at "killing" sticks. R. MEARNS

These two youngsters are so close together they almost look like one bird. The winglike shape at the right is actually a second chick's well-feathered tail. © WAYNE LYNCH

As the chicks grow up, they become more intimidating, even to their parents, which sometimes seem reluctant to bring food to the nest. R. WAYNE NELSON

When the nestlings are tiny, their parents prepare food for them with great delicacy. Here, a female falcon brings prey to a "plucking post," where she will defeather it before taking it to the nest. As the youngsters grow up, the parents are naturally more inclined to let them look out for themselves. But they do not leave them entirely on their own. Though they no longer serve them plucked baby food, they continue to provide food for their young for up to two months after they leave the nest. RICHARD FYFE

Left: An adult peregrine hands a pigeon to a recently fledged youngster. Parents not only transfer food in midair, like this, but also fly above their airborne young and drop dead birds in front of them, as if trying to teach them to strike at moving targets. ROBERT GALBRAITH

Bottom left: Peregrines usually make their first flight when they are about five or six weeks old, with the males taking the leap before the females. Some are daring fliers from the moment they launch, but even the bravest and best of them are less skilled than adults. It may take them a year or more to master the arts of the hunt. LEN RUE, JR.

Although tufts of down on its back and head bear witness to its youth, this falcon is full grown and ready to strike out on its own. This bird is a member of an exceptionally dark population of peregrines in the southern Andes Mountains. DAVID H. ELLIS

As the wind ripples around its neck, a recently fledged peregrine calls for someone to take pity and bring it something to eat. Although it looks rather formidable, this youngster is actually very vulnerable to bad luck, bad weather and, especially, its own inexperience. Only about half of the peregrines that fledge make it to their first birthday, and fewer still reach maturity in the following year. These high natural losses also take their toll on captive-bred youngsters once they are out in the wild, so dozens of young birds must be released in order to establish each new breeding pair.
LAYNE KENNEDY

Above and bottom right: *A peregrine wears its handsome "teenaged" plumage until the spring or summer of its second year, when it moults and puts on adult garb. The robust-looking creature above is an immature female. Young males, like the bird shown bottom right, are more svelte than the females but are otherwise similar.*
JORMA LUHTA

Right: *Once they are on the wing, peregrines from subpolar regions have little time to test their powers or enjoy their summer homes before facing the challenge of migration, alone. Some travel relatively short distances, but others span half the globe—one-way flights of 14 000 kilometres (about 9000 miles) or more are not unknown. Unhappily, these odysseys still take many unwitting peregrines straight into DDT danger zones.*
JORMA LUHTA

POISONED PROSPECTS

"THE OBLIGATION TO ENDURE GIVES US THE RIGHT
TO KNOW."

—Jean Rostand

A cross the river, on the very rooftop where I had seen my first peregrine, a gate opens and a man

lets himself over the wall. He dangles across a steep glass face and scrambles into a window well

outside the twenty-fourth floor. Only a knee-high railing screens the drop to the street.

Above the climber, peering over the edge, are more men, some with TV cameras poised to record his descent.

And above them, in the air, hang two peregrines, the sturdy, wide-winged female and her more delicate mate. At

first both falcons seem 'relaxed, wheeling in large, easy loops, but when the man reaches the window well, they

cut in tightly over his head and start to scream.

I am at my usual post on the riverbank, peering up through binoculars, but the calls carry across the water, a

shrill, irritated, furious, relentless bombardment of sound. Ka-ka-ka-ka-kak. And even though I can't see every-

thing that is happening behind the rail, I know why the birds are alarmed. The man is standing in the cranny

where they have scraped out a nest. At his feet sprawl three young falcon chicks, little round-eyed balls of fluff,

all bellies, beaks and claws.

Last year, when a similar scene was played out, there had only been one youngster in the falcons' nest, but

when the climber left and the birds returned to their ledge, they found their family had suddenly grown to four.

Though the peregrines could scarcely have understood, the three extra youngsters had been hatched in captivity, carried in by the climber and left for the falcons to raise. At first the adult birds hung back, uncertain what to make of this daunting gift, but they soon recovered from their shock and spent the rest of the summer hunting to keep the family fed. That fall, four well-fed young falcons flew from the rooftops and headed south to their wintering grounds in Central and South America.

This year, with three chicks of their own, the adult falcons already have their work cut out for them, and the climber has not brought them any more. All he wants to do is band their babies and leave. But the falcons, aware only of the danger to their young, are now in a total uproar. They scream and circle; they dive. First one, then the other climbs the sky and launches itself like a missile towards the window well. The intruder doubles over, his face down and his back to his birds; he looks awkwardly over his shoulder to see what is coming at him. Again and again the falcons plunge, within inches of his skin—yet somehow, at the last instant, they zip past, carve a hairpin bend and tear up and away without touching him.

"It's pretty exciting," says Paddy Thompson, who has supervised the banding trip, when I speak to him afterwards. But what he has in mind is not the rush of the falcons' aggressive flight. Instead, he is thinking of the simple fact that the pair has hatched more young this year than ever before. Three chicks is a healthy, normal brood, a number that bodes well for the future. Last year, with its single chick, and the year before, with none, had raised anxious doubts. Perhaps the male and female were not compatible, or the female was too old to produce well (no one knew her history). Or worst of all,

maybe she had been poisoned by DDT and could not breed properly.

It is frustrating that even now—twenty years after DDT was blacklisted in Canada, the United States and most of western Europe—there is still reason to worry about peregrines' reproductive health. Even now, peregrines from many parts of the world carry worrisome amounts of DDT and other organochlorines in their bodies. For example, although the pair in Saskatoon appears to be healthy, the same cannot be said for some birds that nest in the neighbouring province of Alberta. There, attempts to reintroduce peregrines were suspended from 1985 to 1991 because the birds were too badly contaminated to reproduce normally. Although pesticide levels are now thought to have declined to safe levels, females that nest in Edmonton and Calgary still produce very few offspring.

Bad enough that this should happen in the city. It is even more upsetting to know that many wilderness falcons also continue to be contaminated. One of the densest and most vigorous peregrine populations in the world lives in the Canadian Arctic, on the rocky western coastline of Hudson Bay near the Inuit village of Rankin Inlet. Well beyond the end of all northward-reaching roads and separated from the nearest farm or factory by an almost unimaginable expanse of tundra and forest, these falcons produce large, healthy broods and give every impression of being in good shape overall. Yet when biologists study the birds' blood and measure the thickness of their eggshells, the results are disquieting. "DDE in blood plasma [and] in the contents of eggs," says a 1990 report. "Residues of a number of other organochlorine pesticides and

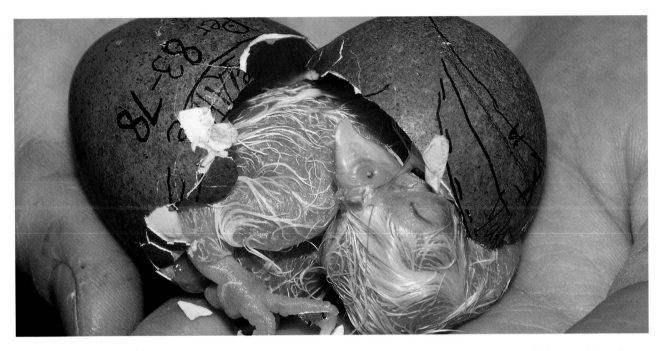

People have done more for the peregrine than for any other endangered species, yet the root cause of their problems has still not been seriously addressed. RICHARD FYFE

polychlorinated biphenyls" (PCBS). Worst of all, eggshells that are within 1 per cent of the "thinning level" at which the population is likely to fail. Though the findings are better than they would have been ten years ago, they are still not reassuring.

How can this be, twenty years after the DDT problem was loudly and publicly "solved"? Why is it that peregrines in southern Finland, for example, are still not able to breed adequately, or that eggs collected on California's Big Sur coast are so hot with toxins that their contents have to be handled with gloves? Where are the poisons coming from?

The answers, as usual, are complex. In some places—California being the prime example—the DDT has hung around in the environment ever

since it was put there in the 1950s and 1960s. Chemical stability was one of the characteristics that made DDT so attractive as an insect poison in the first place: it was not easily broken down by sun, wind, rain or biological activity, and it could go on killing pests for months after it was applied. As it turned out, DDT that washed down into the soil or settled into sediments on the ocean floor has persisted for decades. Its half life in soil has recently been estimated at about sixty years. In most places, the amount of pesticide that trickles out of these hidden deposits is too small to cause obvious harm, but where the concentrations are significant, so are the consequences. Off the coast of southern California, for example, where pesticide manufacturers formerly flushed hundreds of tonnes of

DDT effluent into the sea—one plant pumped out almost 300 kilograms (600 pounds) a day—the level of contamination has still not begun to decrease. And now new micropollutants, including dioxins, are being added to the toxic soup that is sucked up through the food chain, from plankton to fish to sea birds to peregrines. On the aeries, falcons incubate lifeless eggs, and even in the laboratory 60 per cent of Big Sur eggs cannot be made to hatch.

It could be worse. At least with this kind of after-the-fact, "hot spot" pollution, the effects are generally local rather than global, and the damage can be expected to diminish with time, as the DDT in the sediments is gradually released and broken down. But there is another source of pollution that is more troubling in the long run. This is the continuing, day-to-day application of DDT and other "compounds of extinction" in Central and South America, Africa, India and other parts of the Third World. Even after the use of organochlorines was restricted in the First World, it remained legal for companies to manufacture the chemicals for export or to produce and sell them offshore. So when markets for DDT dried up in the wealthy countries, the manufacturers promptly offered their wonder-working pesticide—proven effective, nontoxic to humans and, above all, cheap—to the "developing" nations, as a weapon in their struggle against hunger and disease. As a result, the use of DDT simply shifted south.

It is tempting to see these events in terms of Good Guys and Bad Guys, with the pesticide companies cast as heartless, moustache-twirling villains with an unholy allegiance to the bottom line. The realities of twentieth-century capitalism being what they are, there is something to be said for this view. What's more, this interpretation has the undoubted attraction that it lets the rest of us off the hook, without having to accept any responsibility for what is happening. But in the final analysis, this stance is not convincing. First World chemical companies are agents of our society and are subject, as corporate citizens, to law and public pressure. If they are continuing to traffic in DDT (and other pesticides that are banned at home), it is partly because we, as a society, permit them to get away with it. Our unwillingness to curb the global sale of DDT and other hazardous pesticides—*and to work with Third World nations to find affordable alternatives*—represents a failure of public understanding, public sentiment and public will.

Nobody knows how much DDT is now being applied to the forests, swamps, farms and cotton plantations of the Third World. Though the volume may be decreasing, it still totals several million kilograms per year. (Mexico, one of the few countries for which figures are available, alone accounts for about 4 million kilograms or 9 million pounds a year.) Nor can anyone predict exactly what the ecological consequences of its application will be. Even now, new and unexpected aspects of the problem keep surfacing. For example, the World Health Organization (WHO) has recently raised an alarm about the effects of DDT on green algae, the single-celled plants that form the basis of aquatic and marine food chains. As little as one part per billion of DDT—an amount equivalent to a grain of sand in an Olympic-sized swimming pool—has been shown to stop growth and photosynthesis in these humble but all-important plants. For this reason alone, "DDT and its metabolites should be regarded as a major environmental hazard," the WHO concludes.

And what of the Third World falcons? What is happening to them? The honest answer is that no one knows. Scientists used to think that DDT was safe to use in the tropics because it decomposed more quickly there than in cooler climates. They predicted that if pesticides did persist in the food chain, the amount would be too small to cause problems for peregrines and other predatory birds. Recent first reports from South America tend to bear this out: peregrine falcon populations appear to be stable, and contaminant levels quite low. But information coming out of Africa gives the story a different twist. Writing under the headline "Poisoned prey in the heart of Africa," researcher Humphrey Crick reports in a recent issue of *New Scientist* that DDT levels in at least six species are high enough to cause population failures. Among the threatened predators are the black sparrowhawk, the African fish eagle and the peregrine.

And that is not the end of the trouble. The use of DDT in Africa and the American tropics has also created a hazard for falcons that nest at the other end of the globe, in the northerly regions of the northern hemisphere. Unlike other peregrines, these falcons are migratory. Every autumn, when the north wind doth blow, the falcons of Scandinavia, northern Russia and China, Canada and the northern United States swing south towards the tropics, and some inevitably and unknowingly head for areas that are sprayed with DDT. So do many of the songbirds, shore birds and other migratory species on which the peregrines prey. When these prey species head north in the spring, they carry the poisons back in their bodies, so peregrines may pick up polluted food at any time of the year. Happily, DDT levels in prey are gradually coming down in most areas, as organochlorines are increasingly replaced by "modern" pesticides. But meanwhile the falcons of Alberta, Rankin Inlet and southern Finland, among others, are still being put at risk.

If the peregrine falcon crisis offered us a lesson on the perils of DDT, we have clearly not taken it in. Nor have we heard the larger message—that any synthetic poison has the potential to wreak capricious damage on the living world. We simply do not have the money, time, skill or knowledge to predict and test for all the possible direct and indirect effects of every new pesticide before it goes into use. We weren't able to do this kind of exhaustive research in the 1940s when DDT was introduced, and we still can't in the 1990s, when some 63,000 chemicals are on the market and up to 1000 new formulations go on sale each year.

When DDT and the other organochlorines were restricted in the First World, we had a choice. We could have set to work wholeheartedly to develop alternatives to chemical pest control. We could have followed what Rachel Carson, in 1962, was already mapping out as "The Other Road." Instead, we reached onto the laboratory shelf for another kind of insect killer. For the organochlorines, a product of Allied wartime research, we substituted a group of chemicals known as carbamates and another family of compounds called organophosphates, which had been developed by the German military in their search for chemical weapons. To these insect poisons we then added a bewildering diversity of weed killers and fungicides.

The dangers associated with the newer pesticides tend to be different from those that came with DDT. For example, present-day insect poisons usually break down quickly after they are applied. Though freaky things can happen and surprise problems occur, it is rare for these compounds to persist as poisons for more than a few weeks. They shouldn't be around to cause trouble for our grandchildren. Similarly, and again because they break down readily, the new chemicals seldom build up in the food chain and endanger predators.

(One of several exceptions is an insecticide called famphur, which is poured on the hides of cattle to kill warble flies. Lamentably, it also kills the magpies that hang around the cows and, then, the hawks and owls that feed on the dead magpies. Bald eagles that scavenge on live-stock carcasses may also die. Although famphur poisoning of raptors is known to be widespread in the United States, no one can say how seri-ous the problem is. Is the harm limited to the suffering of individual birds (which may be un-acceptable but at least is not catastrophic), or are whole populations, or species, being threat-ened? No one knows, and as researcher Charles Henny reports, with a rasp of frustration that can be heard through the deadpan of his scientific prose, "effort to pursue . . . detection [of the problem] has been nearly nonexistent." What's more, a solution is within easy reach—we could stop using pour-on products and switch to those, just as effective, that can be given to cattle internally.)

Although the threat of secondary poisoning of raptors may still be too great, the newer insect poisons are clearly less dangerous than the organochlorines, in that they break down more rapidly. But in other ways, present-day chemi-cals may actually be worse than the products they replaced. Unlike DDT, for example, many modern insecticides are highly poisonous—knockdown, drop-dead poisonous—to warm-

blooded creatures. A single granule of car-bofuran, for example, an insect poison that is widely used in North America, will kill a bird the size of a starling. One expert estimates the death toll from granular insecticides, in the corn belt of Ontario, Canada, alone, at 200,000 birds per year. And in Africa, Humphrey Crick calcu-lates that the dosage of fenitrothion used against locusts during a recent, internationally financed campaign was strong enough to kill almost all of the birds that were caught in the spray.

Not every application of insecticide results in this kind of destruction. The harm to bird life depends on two factors: how much of the chemical is applied and how much of this dosage the birds are ultimately exposed to. If, for example, a carefully regulated amount of pesticide is sprayed by tractor onto bare land, where birds have no reason to go, the chemical may do its work and break down without caus-ing obvious harm. But if it is laid on the soil in the form of seedlike granules, which attract graniverous birds; or sprayed from an airplane onto shrubs and hedgerows where songbirds have their nests; or applied to hay fields where grouse go to feed, then the results can be disas-trous.

Again, our ignorance about the consequences of these losses is significant. "The long-term ef-fects of OP[organophosphate]-related mortality on wildlife populations are not known," re-searchers bluntly admit. They are equally unsure what to make of the so-called "sublethal" ef-fects, which show up in birds that survive a pesticide attack. Because modern insecticides are nerve poisons, they can cause a bizarre array of symptoms, including loss of appetite, blurred vision, poor hearing, reduced resistance to dis-ease and impaired learning ability. They can

Burrowing owls, already endangered by a loss of habitat, seem also to be falling victim to an insect poison called carbofuran. ARTHUR SAVAGE

addle the structure of a bird's song or muddle its reflexes so that it fails to feed its nestlings. Sometimes these disabilities persist for many weeks, but usually the bird recovers within a few hours or days. Still, long-term damage can be done if the bird or its young become sickly and weak because of the poisoning.

On the one hand, then, many of the insecticides in use today can harm birds (both as individuals and as species) by direct poisoning, whether that results in illness or causes immediate death. Theoretically, the worst of these problems can be solved by outlawing the most dangerous uses of the most dangerous pesticides: famphur as a pour-on, carbofuran in pellets and sprays, diazinon on turf and so on. In practice, even after the hazard is recognized, it may take decades of wearisome, legalistic

wrangling before the regulations are changed and the poisonings finally stop. In the cases of famphur, carbofuran and diazinon, for example, harmful applications are still permitted in North America, though the danger they pose to bird life has been known for years.

Obviously, it would help if these abuses were stopped, but even that would not be enough to solve the problem we face. The fundamental problem posed by pesticides (insect poisons, weed killers and fungicides combined) is not just that they can knock off choice populations or species, as they almost did with the peregrine. It is that they weaken and impoverish whole ecosystems. Take the case of the grey partridge, for example. Once the most common game bird in the British Isles, its population plummeted because of pesticide use. But the cause was not direct poisoning; instead, the chain of effects was devious. The process began with the application of a "safe," nontoxic herbicide to the fields to kill weeds. As might have been predicted, this had no effect on the partridges, but it did, of course, thin out the number of broadleaf plants. And that's where the trouble began. Fewer plants meant less food for beetles, bugs and caterpillars; fewer insects meant less food for the partridge chicks in the spring. The partridge chicks starved, and the population crashed.

The vast North American prairie, with its millions of potholes and sloughs, is the "duck factory" of the western hemisphere. But in recent years, the factory has been on slowdown and the populations of several species of waterfowl have dropped to the lowest levels ever known. Why is this happening? Overhunting? Drought? The continuing loss of wetlands to the seed drill? All of these processes may play a part. But many researchers suspect that pesticides are also involved. Herbicides that leach into ponds and marshes may wipe out water plants; insecticides kill other pond life. At a time when wetlands are shrinking and the ducks have fewer places to go, the quality of their habitat—its ability to provide shelter and food—is also deteriorating. Maybe this explains why the few ponds that remain are not filled with ducks, as they would have been in earlier decades.

In Britain, where bird populations may be more closely studied than anywhere else in the world, researchers are now reporting an "alarming" decline. "More of the most common species have gone down rather than up in numbers" in the last thirty years, according to a 1990 report from the British Trust for Ornithology. Other studies echo this message: lapwings have been reduced by about 30 per cent since the mid-1970s and song thrushes by half; linnets have declined by a quarter and are losing more than a third of their chicks to starvation. Once again, pesticides are implicated, but often in a most indirect way. In the final analysis, the blame rests with the ultraspecialized, ultraefficient method of farming that pesticides permit. Chemical agriculture has redesigned and streamlined the entire farm landscape. Until quite recently, farmers controlled pests with crop rotations and seasonal cultivations, techniques that helped to maintain diversity in the farm ecosystem and provide a mix of habitats for wild creatures. But with the widespread acceptance of pesticides, these life-enhancing practices were abandoned, and with them went the birds.

The situation would be unbearable were it not for one fact. We do have alternatives; we do not have to go on clubbing the Earth to death with these brutal technologies. We know, from studies that have now been conducted in several parts of the world, that "organic" farms, where food is grown with little or no pesticide, support significantly more birds and more bird species than those on which pesticides are used. We know, from a book-length study entitled *Alternative Agriculture* published in 1989 by the National Research Council of the United States, that low-pesticide and no-pesticide farming can be highly productive and highly profitable. We know, from the example of Sweden, which is well on its way to a 50 per cent reduction in pesticide use, that people and nations can decide to stand on the side of life.

As Rachel Carson told us,

> The choice . . . is ours to make. If, having endured much, we have at last asserted our "right to know," and if, knowing, we have concluded that we are being asked to take senseless and frightening risks, then we should no longer accept the counsel of those who tell us that we must fill our world with poisonous chemicals; we should look about and see what other course is open to us.

We know which road we must take. And that road takes us back to the peregrine falcon again, back through the lessons of the recent past and, farther still, back to the message of hope that the falcon has long been empowered to bring. "Peregrines are birds that stretch the imagination," somebody said to me, and with imagination comes hope. We are not trapped by the past. We can create the future we need, under the falcon's wing.

The peregrine is often portrayed as the hero of an ecological success story. A species that seemed to be on a collision course with extinction is alive, and its numbers grow larger each year! Better yet, we humans can claim a share of the credit, because we are helping to bring the falcons back in many parts of the world. It's like a burst of sunlight in the ecological gloom, and we are understandably tempted to make the most of it. JORMA LUHTA

As soon as DDT and other harmful compounds were restricted, peregrines spontaneously began to rebound in many areas. In southern Scotland, for example (as in much of Great Britain), there are now more peregrines than ever before. One reason for the quick turnaround of British peregrines is that there were always a few falcons left. As soon as these survivors were able to raise chicks again, a new generation of falcons flew out and resettled the vacant cliffs. R. MEARNS

The peregrine recovery in most countries has been less exuberant and complete than in Britain. Overall, however, the trends are promising. As the levels of organochlorine pollution have come down in the last twenty years, the numbers of peregrines have risen reciprocally.

Not surprisingly, the recovery has been weakest in areas where the losses were most devastating. In eastern Europe and eastern North America, for example, the decline was so drastic and the regions affected so vast that the falcons have not been able to come back by themselves. There simply weren't enough of them left to repopulate the empty landscape. That's why captive-breeding programs, which have sent waves of young falcons out into the wild, have been such an important factor in the peregrine's return.

Organizations that have bred peregrines for release include the World Center for Birds of Prey in Boise, Idaho; Cornell University in Ithaca, New York; the Santa Cruz Predatory Bird Research Group in California; the Canadian Wildlife Service; the Swedish Society for the Conservation of Nature, and the Deutscher Falkenorden. STEPHEN J. KRASEMANN/VALAN PHOTOS

Since captive-breeding began, peregrines have taken up residence in more than two dozen cities, where they add a spark of wildness to the skyline.

Often, these city-dwellers are birds that were hatched in captivity and released from the rooftops. Raising the birds in the city has several advantages. For one thing, it's cheaper to work in town than to set up camp in the back country. For another, urban releases have brought the peregrine and its message into millions of people's lives. JON TRIFFO

Since peregrines have taken up residence in our habitat, we have enjoyed a privileged view of their intimate lives. Here, a male peregrine woos his mate with a gift of food on a Montreal high-rise. ROBERT GALBRAITH

Peregrines have personality. Here, a two-year-old peregrine makes a fearless assault on the rooftops of Regina, Saskatchewan. In a gentler mood, this young bird inexplicably decided to take on the task of hunting for a batch of captive-bred falcon chicks that were being prepared for release. JON TRIFFO

Not all city people (nor all people anywhere) are happy about the peregrines' resurgence. In California, for example, several peregrines have been shot, and a pigeon keeper was convicted and fined in one instance. In parts of Europe, disturbance of nests by climbers, photographers and developers is a continuing problem, as are thefts of young birds. SEPPO SAARI
Right: "Don't talk to me. Don't even look at me." This indignant-looking falcon is not really in a bad mood. Instead, it has settled into a daze after a heavy meal. Many urban peregrines feed mainly on pigeons, a species that seldom carries DDT residues. So, despite the inevitable hazards of urban life, city-nesting peregrines are generally very successful. JON TRIFFO

Although city-nesting falcons get most of the limelight, hundreds of peregrines have also been established on wilderness aeries, both with and without human help. There are now over 4000 pairs in Europe and more than 1200 in North America, a four-fold increase in the last twenty years. © WAYNE LYNCH

Left: *A peregrine rides the updraft over the "cliffs" of Los Angeles.* GALEN ROWELL/MOUNTAIN LIGHT

Bottom left: *A peregrine chick at an urban release site contemplates taking a bath.* JON TRIFFO

With the California sunshine spilling over its wings, a peregrine falcon soars above the Big Sur coast. Unhappily, this bird is a member of a population of falcons that is still acutely poisoned with DDT.

    Whether we like it or not, the "happy ending" of the peregrine story is soured by ambiguity. For all the successes of the recovery programs, many populations of peregrines continue to suffer some degree of reproductive disability, because DDT *and other dangerous organochlorines are still present in the biosphere.* GALEN ROWELL/MOUNTAIN LIGHT

A climber removes a fragile egg from an aerie on the Big Sur coast in California. Because the egg would break and die if left in the nest, it will be carried to a laboratory, where it has a chance of hatching. GALEN ROWELL/
MOUNTAIN LIGHT

An infertile peregrine egg from the Big Sur coast, cracked and leaking, 1991. GALEN ROWELL/MOUNTAIN LIGHT

Trays of thin-shelled peregrine eggs that have been incubated by the Santa Cruz Predatory Bird Research Group in California. DDT *contamination has remained high and constant in Big Sur eggs since about 1978, and other pollutants, including dioxins, are now being detected. Nobody knows how these toxins affect peregrines, but they are probably responsible for the recent increase in the number of eggs that fail to hatch.* GALEN ROWELL/MOUNTAIN LIGHT

"Feed me," shouts a chick hatched from a thin-shelled egg at the Santa Cruz laboratory. GALEN ROWELL/ MOUNTAIN LIGHT

A peregrine falcon in California tends its foster family. These little chicks were removed from the nest as eggs, hatched in the laboratory and then carried back into the wild. Yet, despite all this effort, the future of these hatchlings, like that of other peregrines on the California coast, is far from secure. The population would certainly vanish if humans withdrew their help. CRAIG HIMMELWRIGHT

Although few populations of peregrines are as sick as the Big Sur birds, some other coastal falcons show signs of ailing health. In Britain, where the overall recovery has been strong and swift, the coastal areas have never regained their full complement of peregrines, and the southeast coast remains vacant. The reason for this is not known, though marine pollution has been fingered as a probable cause. The crude fact is that, too often, we use the seas as sewers for our chemical effluent.

Halfway around the world, in British Columbia, an especially vigorous population of peregrines once lived on

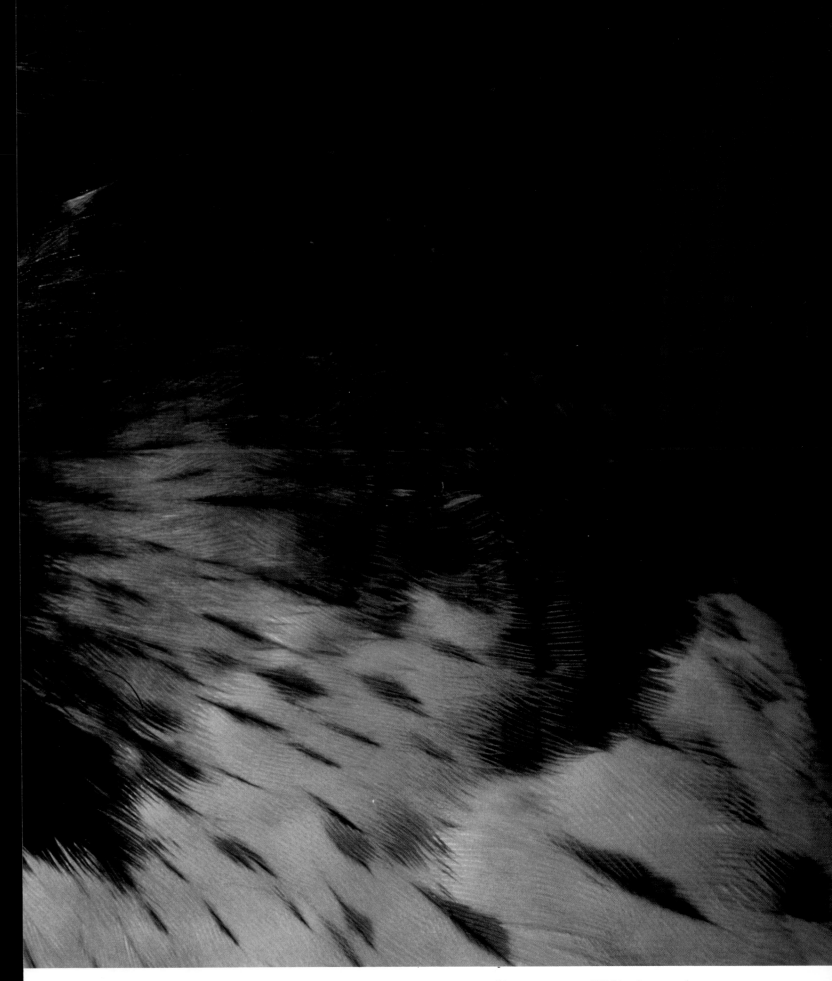

Langara Island in the Queen Charlotte chain. Then, in the late 1950s, something went wrong. Within the span of a decade, the population fell from two dozen pairs to five or six. The cause of this loss was a calamitous decline in the sea birds on which the falcons preyed. But what caused the sea-bird population to crash? Was it predation, as some people think, or something more insidious? JOHN HENDRICKSON

Peregrines that nest in the northern reaches of the world are also especially likely to suffer reproductive problems Sometimes the symptoms are relatively innocuous. For example, the egg from which this little fellow hatched in northern Finland was probably somewhat thinner than it should have been. Still, it was obviously sturdy enough to do its job. But in southern Finland, an average peregrine shell is one-quarter thinner than it ought to be, and the population appears to be in serious trouble. *ABOVE:* HANNU HAUTALA; *RIGHT:* JOUNI RUUSKANEN, FINLAND

In 1981, when biologists first began to study the falcons near Rankin Inlet on the west coast of Hudson Bay, they were amazed. Nobody had ever before seen so many peregrines in such a small area of the far North. Although peregrines often breed several thousand kilometres from their nearest neighbour, here the cliff faces were dotted with nests, each within a few minutes' flight of the next. What's more, most of the breeding pairs were raising big, healthy families.

But not all. Even here, many pairs were showing the all-too-familiar symptoms of DDT poisoning. To this day, one pair in ten is unable to reproduce properly.

MARK BRADLEY

These dead peregrine chicks from the Canadian Arctic are present-day victims of DDT poisoning. Although many thin-shelled eggs break early in incubation, some collapse just as the chicks begin to hatch, like the one on the right. Others, like the one on the left, fail because thin cracks form around the "pip." The egg loses moisture through these fissures, shell membranes shrink around the chick inside, and the youngster dies. GORDON COURT

When it first became clear that peregrines from the wilderness of Alaska, Canada and northern Europe were suffering from DDT poisoning, researchers did not know how the birds were being contaminated. Their best guess was that the falcons and their prey were picking up toxins on their wintering grounds and carrying them north in their bodies in the spring. But they couldn't prove it because (a decade and more after humankind's first step on the moon) nobody knew where these peregrines went for the winter.

Since then thousands of peregrine chicks have been fitted with bands, or rings, in an attempt to learn more about the species' movements. Each band carries coded information about the bird's birthplace. If the falcon dies and the band is recovered on its wintering grounds, researchers get some idea of its travels. RICHARD FYFE

Above: *As far as anyone knows, the peregrines of South America are not showing any ill effects from* DDT *use. But in Africa, peregrines and other predatory birds are thought to be in immediate danger.* DAVID H. ELLIS

Right: *Thanks to the banding program, the "circle of poison" that links North and South has now been proved. Peregrines from northern latitudes, like this dapper tundra bird, often do head into regions where* DDT *and other hazardous organochlorines are still in use. In North America, for example, peregrines winter along the Gulf Coast of the United States, throughout Mexico and Central America, and as far south as Chile and Uruguay. From the U.S. border south,* DDT *is still widely used, even where it is officially restricted or banned.* © WAYNE LYNCH

Bottom right: *A billboard on the Pan-American highway in Ecuador promotes pesticide use. Although world pesticide sales are still concentrated in the industrialized countries, the First World market has levelled off and the Third World is the new growth area for the chemical industry. Given the realities of poverty, illiteracy and inadequate law enforcement in so-called developing countries, the misuse of pesticides is inevitable, and people as well as wildlife suffer.* GALEN ROWELL/MOUNTAIN LIGHT

For thousands of years, the beauty and vitality of peregrine falcons have spoken to humankind. Peregrines have brought us an awareness of the sacred kinship of life.

We must honour this awareness by reducing our dependence on pesticides. At present, human beings disperse about 21.5 billion kilograms (47 billion pounds) of pesticides over the planet each year. Yet the U. S. National Research Council has recently shown that "alternative" farming methods, which require less of both fertilizers and pesticides, are "practical and economical ways to maintain yields, conserve soil, maintain water quality, and lower operating costs." Integrated Pest Management, a methodology that relies on pesticides only as a last resort, has proven highly effective in places as diverse as Canada, California and Indonesia. We know what we have to do, and it's time we did it. *ABOVE:* FRANS LANTING/MINDEN PICTURES; *RIGHT:* GALEN ROWELL/MOUNTAIN LIGHT

Bring us hope, bright falcon. Give us the will to act.
ABOVE: LAYNE KENNEDY; *LEFT:* THOMAS L.
MAECHTLE; *BOTTOM LEFT:* RICHARD FYFE

REFERENCES

To learn more about the international efforts to oppose the unnecessary use of pesticides, contact the Pesticide Action Network at the address closest to you.

Africa: Environment Liaison Centre International, P. O. Box 72461, Nairobi, Kenya or Environnement et developpement du tiers monde, B. P. 3370, Dakar, Senegal

Asia/Pacific: IOCU Regional Office for Asia and the Pacific, P. O. Box 1045, 10830 Penang, Malaysia

Europe: PAN Europe, Damrak 83-1, 1012 LN Amsterdam, Netherlands

Latin America: Fundacio Natura, Casilla 253, Quito, Ecuador

North America: PAN North America Regional Center, 965 Mission Street #514, San Francisco, CA 94103, U.S.A.

For more information on peregrines and on the effects of pesticides on wildlife, you may wish to consult the publications listed below, which were used in the preparation of this book. The most informative general references are indicated with an asterisk.

Al-Timimi, F. A. 1987. *Falcons and falconry in Qatar*. Doha: Ali Bin Ali Printing Press.

Balcomb, R. 1983. Secondary poisoning of Red-shouldered Hawks with carbofuran. *J. Wildl. Manage.* 47:1129-32.

* Bent, A. C. 1961 (1937). *Life histories of North American birds of prey*, part 2. New York: Dover.

Bijleveld, M. 1974. *Birds of prey in Europe*. London: Macmillan.

Bird, D. M. 1982. Reproductive and hunting behaviour in Peregrine Falcons, *Falco peregrinus*, in Southern Quebec. *Can. Field-Nat.* 96 (2):167-71.

Blus, L. J., et al. 1989. Effects of organophosphorus insecticides on Sage Grouse in southeastern Idaho. *J. Wildl. Manage.* 53:1139-46.

Bonwick, J. 1956. *Egyptian belief and modern thought*. Indian Hills, Colo.: Falcon's Wing Press.

Brewer, L. W., et al. 1988. Effects of methyl parathion in ducks and duck broods. *Envir. Tox. Chem.* 7:375-79.

Burton, D. K., and Philogène, B. 1986. An overview of pesticide usage in Latin America. Unpublished report to the Canadian Wildlife Service Latin American Program.

* Cade, T. J. 1982. *The falcons of the world*. Boise, Idaho: Cornell University Press.

Cade, T. J. 1968. The Gyrfalcon and falconry.

Living Bird 7:237-40.

* Cade, T. J., and Bird, D. M. 1990. Peregrine falcons nesting in an urban environment: A review. *Can. Field-Nat.* 104:209-18.

Cade, T. J.; Enderson, J. H.; Thelander, C. G.; and White, C. M. 1988. *Peregrine falcon populations: Their management and recovery.* Ithaca, N.Y.: The Peregrine Fund Inc.

Cade, T. J.; White, C. M.; and Haugh, J. R. 1968. Peregrines and pesticides in Alaska. *The Condor* 70:170-78.

Carson, R. 1962. *Silent spring.* New York: Crest Books.

Cernetig, M. 1990. Raptor's flight watched with concern. Toronto *Globe and Mail*, August 28.

Clark, T. R. 1959. *Myth and symbol in ancient Egypt.* London: Thames & Hudson.

Corn, P. S.; Stolzenburg, W.; and Bury, R. B. 1989. Acid precipitation studies in Colorado and Wyoming: Interim report of surveys of montane amphibians and water chemistry. U. S. Fish and Wildlife Service Biological Report 80 (40.26).

Court, G. S.; Bradley, D. M.; Gates, C. G.; and Boag, D. A. 1988. Turnover and recruitment in a tundra population of Peregrine Falcons *Falco peregrinus. Ibis* 131:487-96.

Court, G. S.; Gates, C. G.; and Boag, D. A. 1988. Natural history of the Peregrine Falcon in the Keewatin District of the Northwest Territories. *Arctic* 41 (1):17-30.

Dekker, D. 1980. Hunting success rates, foraging habits, and prey selection of Peregrine Falcons migrating through central Alberta. *Can. Field-Nat.* 94:371-82.

Diamond, A. W., and Filion, F. L., eds. 1987. *The value of birds: Proceedings of a workshop, June 1986, Queen's University, Kingston, Ontario.* International Council for Bird Preser-
vation Technical Publication No. 6.

Donigan, A. S., and Carsel, R. F. 1987. Modeling the impact of conservation tillage practices on pesticide concentrations in ground and surface waters. *Envir. Tox. Chem.* 6:241-51.

* Dunlap, T. R. 1981. *DDT: Scientists, citizens, and public policy.* Princeton, N. J.: Princeton University Press.

Dwernychuk, L. W., and Boag, D. A. 1973. Effect of herbicide-induced changes in vegetation on nesting ducks. *Can. Field-Nat.* 87:155-65.

Elliott, J. E.; Butler, R. W.; Norstrom, R. J.; and Whitehead, P. E. 1989. Environmental contaminants and reproductive success of Great Blue Herons *Ardea herodias* in British Columbia, 1986-87. *Environmental Pollution* 59:91-114.

Ellis, D. H. 1985. The austral Peregrine Falcon: Color variation, productivity, and pesticides. *Nat. Geog. Research 1* (3):388-94.

Erickson, G., et al. 1988. Anatum *Peregrine recovery plan.* Western Raptor Technical Committee, Canadian Wildlife Service.

Fairbrother, A.; Meyers, S. M.; and Bennett, R. S. 1988. Changes in Mallard hen and brood behaviors in response to methyl parathion-induced illness of ducklings. *Envir. Tox. Chem.* 7:499-503.

Fletcher, W. W. 1974. *The pest war.* Oxford: Basil Blackwell.

Flickinger, E. L.; King, K. A.; Stout, W. F.; and Mohn, M. M. 1980. Wildlife hazards from Furadan 3G applications to rice in Texas. *J. Wildl. Manage.* 44:190-97.

Flint, M. L., and van den Bosch, R. 1981. *Introduction to integrated pest management.* New York: Plenum Press.

Forsyth, D. J. 1989a. Agricultural chemicals and

prairie pothole wetlands: Meeting the needs
of the resource and the farmer—Canadian
perspective. *Trans. N. A. Wildl. and Nat. Res.
Conf.* 54:59-66.

——. 1989b. Potential effects of pesticides on
wildlife in wetlands. In *Proceedings of the
symposium on water management affecting the
wet-to-dry transition: Planning at the margins,
University of Regina, Nov. 8-9, 1988*, ed. W.
Nicholaichuk and H. Steppuhn, 199-210.

Foundation for Advancements in Science and
Education. 1991. Special report: Exporting
banned and hazardous pesticides, a
preliminary review. *FASE Reports* 9 (1): S1-S8.

Grue, C. E., et al. 1989. Agricultural chemicals
and prairie pothole wetlands: Meeting the
needs of the resource and the farmer—U. S.
perspective. *Trans. N. A. Wildl. and Nat. Res.
Conf.* 54:43-58.

——. 1986. Potential impacts of agricultural
chemicals on waterfowl and other wildlife in-
habiting prairie wetlands: An evaluation of
research needs and approaches. *Trans. N. A.
Wildl. and Nat. Res. Conf.* 51:357-381.

Grue, C. E.; Fleming, W. J.; Busby, D. G.; and
Hill, E. F. 1983. Assessing hazards of
organophosphate pesticides to wildlife. *Trans.
N. A. Wildl. and Nat. Res. Conf.* 48:200-20.

Hall, G. H. 1970. The story of the Sun Life falcons. *Can. Field-Nat.* 84:20-30.

Harris, J. T. 1981. *The Peregrine Falcon in Greenland*. Columbia, Missouri: University of Missouri Press.

Hart, G. 1986. *A dictionary of Egyptian gods and
goddesses*. London: Routledge and Kegan Paul.

Henny, C. J., and Herron, G. B. 1989. DDE,
selenium, mercury, and White-faced Ibis re-
production at Carson Lake, Nevada. *J. Wildl.
Manage.* 53:1032-45.

Henny, C. J.; Kolbe, E. J.; Hill, E. F.; and Blus,
L. J. 1987. Case histories of Bald Eagles and
other raptors killed by organophosphorus insecticides topically applied to livestock. *J.
Wildl. Disease* 23:292-95.

Herbert, R. A., and Herbert, K. G. S. 1965. Be-
havior of Peregrine Falcons in the New York
City region. *Auk*:62-94.

Hickey, J. J. 1970. Peregrine Falcons, pollutants,
and propaganda. *Can. Field-Nat.* 84:207-8.

Hoffman, D. J. 1990. Embryotoxicity and
teratogenicity of environmental contaminants
to bird eggs. *Reviews of Environmental Contamination and Toxicology* 115:39-89.

Hynes, H. P. 1989. *The recurring Silent Spring*.
New York: Pergamon Press.

James, P. C., and Fox, G. A. 1987. Effects of
some insecticides on productivity of burrowing owls. *Blue Jay* 45:65-71.

Johnson, D. H., and Shaffer, T. L. 1987. Are
mallards declining in North America? *Wildlife
Society Bulletin* 15:340-45.

Leary, J. C.; Fishbein, W. I.; and Salter, L. C.
1946. *DDT and the insect problem*. New York:
McGraw-Hill.

Liotta, P. H. 1989. *Learning to fly*. Chapel Hill,
N. C.: Algonquin Books of Chapel Hill.

Meyburg, B.-U., and Chancellor, R. D., eds.
1989. *Raptors in the modern world*. Berlin:
World Working Group on Birds of Prey and
Owls.

Miller, M. W., and Berge, G. C., eds. 1969.
*Chemical fallout: Current research on persistent
pesticides*. Springfield, Ill.: Charles C. Thomas.

Mineau, P. 1988. Avian mortality in agro-
ecosystems. 1. The case against granular insecticides in Canada. In *Field methods for the
study of environmental effects of pesticides*, ed.
M. P. Greaves et al., 3-12. British Crop Pro-

tection Council Monograph No. 40.

* Moriarty, F. 1988. *Ecotoxicology: The study of pollutants in ecosystems*. 2d. ed. London: Academic Press.

* National Research Council. 1989. *Alternative agriculture*. Washington, D. C.: National Academy Press.

* O'Connor, R. J., and Shrubb, M. 1986. *Farming and birds*. Cambridge University Press.

Ottawa Field Naturalists' Club. 1990. Peregrine Falcons in the 1980s (a special issue). *Can. Field-Nat.* 104:167-292.

Pace, C. 1986. EPA prevents DDT from returning in disguise. *Audubon Activist* (Nov.):7.

Peakall, D. B. 1976. The Peregrine Falcon (*Falco peregrinus*) and pesticides. *Can. Field-Nat.* 90:301-7.

Pimentel, D., et al. Environmental and social costs of pesticides. In preparation.

Rands, M., and Sotherton, N. 1985. Pesticides threaten British wildlife. *New Scientist* 4 July, 32.

* Ratcliffe, D. 1980. *The Peregrine falcon*. Vermillion, S. D.: Buteo Books.

Rowell, Galen. 1991. Falcon rescue. *National Geographic* 179 (4):106-15.

Schwarzbach, S. E.; Shull, L.; and Grau, C. R. 1988. Eggshell thinning in ring doves exposed to p,p' Dicofol. *Arch. Environ. Contam. Toxicol.* 17:219-27.

Shank, C. C.; Bromley, R. B.; and Poole, K. G. *Numerical changes in two breeding populations of tundra Peregrine Falcons in the central Canadian Arctic*. In press.

Stevens, R. 1975. *The taming of Genghis*. Saskatoon, Sask.: Falconiforme Press.

Terborgh, J. 1989. *Where have all the birds gone?* Princeton, N. J.: Princeton University Press.

Watterson, B. 1984. *The gods of ancient Egypt*. London: B. T. Batsford.

World Health Organization. 1989. *DDT and its derivatives—Environmental aspects*. Environmental Health Criteria 83.

INDEX